Cultivating an
Entrepreneurial Mindset

Cultivating an Entrepreneurial Mindset

Tamiko L. Cuellar

BEP BUSINESS EXPERT PRESS

First published in 2019 by
Business Expert Press, LLC
222 East 46th Street, New York, NY 10017
www.businessexpertpress.com

ISBN-13: 978-1-94858-076-2 (paperback)
ISBN-13: 978-1-94858-075-5 (e-book)

Business Expert Press Entrepreneurship and Small Business Management Collection

Collection ISSN: 1946-5653 (print)
Collection ISSN: 1946-5661 (electronic)

Cover and interior design by S4Carlisle Publishing Services Private Ltd., Chennai, India
Cover image by Nizwa Design/shutterstock.com

First edition: 2019

10 9 8 7 6 5 4 3 2 1

Printed in the United States of America.

Advanced Quotes for *Cultivating an Entrepreneurial Mindset*

Tamiko Cuellar shows the importance of having 12 specific mindsets to have entrepreneurial success. As a successful entrepreneur herself, Tamiko speaks from experience in very practical terms. This book helps explain the mindsets of how entrepreneurs see the world that makes them successful. It is a great book for anyone seeking practical tips on how you can develop your own mindset to be more successful as an entrepreneur.

Dr. Andrew Sears
President of City Vision University, USA

A great supplement to anyone considering entrepreneurship! Insightful and compelling stories with practical exercises and assessments! A lived experience by Cuellar, on how "mindset will either create obstacles or opportunities, see barriers or possibilities and cause fear or courage". A must read for students studying entrepreneurship and truly wants to cultivate an entrepreneurial mindset.

Dr. Mauvalyn M. Bowen
Associate Professor of Business & Entrepreneurship
Bethel University, USA

Tamiko Cuellar brilliantly tackles the 12 types of mindsets that are crucial to think like an entrepreneur. As an entrepreneur and a PhD business student, I now understand the importance of training the mind in order to operate at your full potential. I'm literally eating these pages up! Absolutely amaaaazing!

Tresia Auala
Project Coordinator for the Entrepreneurship
and Incubation Programme
University of Namibia Business School, Namibia

In line with the author's mission to help individuals discover and pursue their life's purpose, Tamiko presents another "best-seller" which should be found in every university's library and curriculum. Tamiko, in her trademark style of authenticity and simplicity, walks the reader through a self-discovery process, where they learn how to identify and utilize, attributes of a "winning entrepreneur." I'm sure an emerging entrepreneur at any stage will identify themselves in many of the scenarios found within the book, which makes it a "must read"!

Adjoa Agyeman
Curriculum & Content Coordinator
Young African Leadership Initiative (YALI), Ghana

Abstract

This book is based on the 12 critical areas of focus for preparing the mind to think like an entrepreneur. Executives, leaders, aspiring entrepreneurs, emerging business owners, and students will be challenged to compare and contrast how their mindsets measure up in each of the 12 areas discussed in the book. Throughout the book are mindset exercises, assessments, and questions to ponder to allow the reader to interact with the content and apply the concepts immediately. The content is substantiated with real-world application of the 12 areas of focus by actual examples of businesses and entrepreneurs who have put into action each of the 12 entrepreneurial mindset focus areas. Readers will take away practical action items to cultivate entrepreneurial thinking and experience a paradigm shift from an employee mindset to an entrepreneurial mindset.

Keywords

Entrepreneurship; mindset; paradigm shift; business ownership; perspective; risk; leadership vision; pioneer; obstacles; change; failure; success; work purpose; uncertainty, status quo; sales; business; startup

Contents

Acknowledgments

Writing a book is truly my labor of love and my present to the world. One of the dearest gifts that the Creator has bestowed upon me is the gift to express literature on pages. Every book that I write, including this one, is a part of the legacy that I would like to leave my family members for generations, present and future, to see and be proud of. People like me from impoverished urban environments don't often make it to the world stage to publish significant works that are seen and read all around the globe. For this, I am eternally grateful.

I am thankful to my mother for doing all she could to see that my gifts and talents were nurtured. Thank you to all of my teachers, academic and spiritual advisors who cared enough to guide me on the path of discovering my calling to the marketplace. This book is made possible in part by what they've imparted into my life.

To my publisher, Business Experts Press (BEP), I am grateful for the professionalism and for flexibility as it helped me with completing this project in between traveling throughout Africa teaching master classes and on a media tour. I have enjoyed working with the team and look forward to a long and prosperous relationship. I am grateful to everyone who contributed any of their time and talents to making this book happen.

And last, but certainly not least—to my family, Mama (Paula), Dad (Robert), Sissy (Mia), my brothers Robert and Quinton, and cousin Cardiesse—thank you all for the support you've given me, both big and small, and for believing in me. You all were the first to know of my dreams, and I appreciate you all for listening. Having you all in my life is a God-send and just knowing that you all are there is a source of comfort for me in this world. Family is everything to me. God has great things in store for the Veal family, and I can't wait to see what each of us will do next to leave our mark on this world!

Introduction

Having been an employee and now an entrepreneur for most of my adult life, I have observed a stark contrast between how employees think and how entrepreneurs think. This book will peel the covers back to give you a rare peek into the inner workings of the mind of an entrepreneur and what you can do to cultivate an entrepreneurial mindset.

My Personal Mindset Journey as an Entrepreneur

I did not set out to become an entrepreneur. It was almost like entrepreneurship chose me. A combination of my personality, work habits and preferences, desired lifestyle, and a few other factors led me down the path of starting my own business. However, it was ultimately my entrepreneurial way of thinking that has sustained me and kept me on this path for most of my adult life, or I would have quit a long time ago! I have always had a natural propensity towards leading rather than following. I would rather tell others what to do rather than be told what to do. Punching the clock daily was never appealing to me. Work for me must be satisfying and personally fulfilling or I'll lose interest. I master things quickly and wanted to create my own fast track to success on my terms rather than wait around for promotions to happen. And finally, the type of wealth that I envisioned for myself was likely not going to be achieved by working for someone else.

I probably came into this world somewhat hardwired for entrepreneurship, but not everyone has to be. Most of what I share with you in this book can be cultivated with the right thinking. Your mind is like a garden. Rich fertilizer, pulling up weeds, and watering are necessary components to produce a flourishing garden. Feeding your mind with beneficial thoughts and eliminating the bad ones are what will help to produce a thriving business. Getting rid of the fear of taking risks and living outside of your comfort zone require a major shift in thinking for many aspiring and emerging entrepreneurs.

Make no mistake. Although I already had a few advantages, I had plenty of mindset obstacles to overcome prior to launching my own businesses. I grew very poor and my family was dependent on government assistance and subsidies for most of my childhood. For a long time, I never saw anyone successful—in my neighborhood or my family—because I was born into a long line of generational poverty. Then, my aunt opened a restaurant where I worked as a teenager. She ran that business for over 30 years and was my first example of a successful entrepreneur. Later, I also witnessed my uncle running a successful restaurant for many years. Shortly after I graduated with my first degree in Business Management, my older sister started a real estate investment business. All three of these family members served as great examples that I didn't initially realize how much I so desperately needed to see after living in such impoverished conditions.

You Are How You Think

Have you ever heard the phrase, "as a man thinketh, so is he?" It is true, although it is not intended to be gender specific. You are the sum of your thoughts. Your very being is tied to what and how you think. This is why it is so important that you guard what I call the gate of your mind. Just as I make every effort to avoid feeding my natural body junk, I make an effort to avoid filling my mind with worthless or detrimental things. There are some thoughts that should not be invited and other thoughts that come that we have to make a conscious effort to reject, also known as casting down vain imaginations.

If you've ever wondered why people meditate, one reason is to reject unwanted thoughts. Meditation also teaches you how to deeply and intentionally focus on thoughts that are good, pure, and lovely. You can meditate on the life you want, the type of person you'd like to become, the success you want to achieve in your business, and any other good thing that you want to accomplish. Meditation will calm your mind and help you to gain clarity of thought, peace, and declutter your mental space from all unnecessary or unfruitful thoughts. It doesn't have anything to do with being religious necessarily; it is about training your mind.

Success starts in the mind. Mindset is a set of beliefs that you hold, which influences your convictions, your decisions, and, ultimately, the direction of your life. Beliefs lead to actions. Your mindset will create obstacles or opportunities, see barriers or possibilities, and cause fear or courage. Your frame of mind started developing from the moment you were born, if not sooner while you were in your mother's womb. The environment in which you were raised, your experiences, and what you have been taught are all factors that shape your thinking. If you've had a barrage of negative experiences in your life that have adversely impacted you, don't feel disheartened. The good news is that your thinking can be rewired to change what you believe - starting by changing what you believe about yourself. The focus within this book is primarily on the actions you can take to cultivate an entrepreneurial mindset to prepare you to make the shift from thinking like an employee to thinking like an entrepreneur.

In the garden of your mind, plucking the weeds of negative thinking that are counterproductive to becoming a great entrepreneur is a must if you expect to succeed as an entrepreneur. A few examples of these "weeds" are having a normalized view of working for someone else, esteeming your comfort zone higher than your dream of becoming an entrepreneur, and perceiving risk as something negative. Your journey as you read this book will help you not only to reflect on your thinking patterns but also to identify unhealthy thinking and replace it with a mindset that is conducive to succeeding as an entrepreneur. But first, you must take an honest assessment of how you think of yourself.

Examining How You Think about Yourself

Before you venture into the world of entrepreneurship, it would be well worth it to dissect how and what you think of yourself. You filter how you view the world and even yourself through your lenses. *Questions to ponder:* How would you describe yourself? Courageous or fearful? Gutsy or timid? Follower of the masses or marching to the beat of your own drum? Tenacious or easily moved?

It matters how you see yourself because that is the lens through which you see the world around you. Thoughts are extremely powerful.

They are the fundamental building blocks to your success as an entrepreneur. Entrepreneurship can sometimes be a lonely journey, so a healthy dose of self-affirmation is needed. Before you can become a successful entrepreneur, you first have to see yourself as one. If you have experienced trauma in your life that you believe might be negatively affecting your perception of yourself, seeing a therapist or counselor can help you work through deeply rooted issues. You could have the most brilliant mind, be highly skilled, and have amazing qualities to run a business, but mindset blockages can hinder you from reaching your ultimate potential.

When I think about myself, I think that I am extremely resilient, laser-focused on my goals, ambitious, loyal, wise, capable, self-reflective, pensive, curious, intelligent, valuable, and inquisitive, among many other things. There are many things that I am not, but I don't dwell on those things. I only choose to think about myself in a positive light despite my awareness of my shortcomings. I have to be aware of my shortcomings for the sole purpose of working to overcome them in order to become a better person, but not to beat myself up or get down on myself.

Why Is It Important to Shift Your Thinking?

Well, if you want to think like an entrepreneur, it's necessary to shift your thinking. Many educational systems globally are structured to teach students to gain a sufficient level of mastery in a particular area of study to prepare them to join the workforce as an employee at someone else's company. There is an invisible yet direct school-to-work pipeline that exists to convert students into workers. The vast majority of the world is indoctrinated in this type of educational system, which has become the societal norm. As stated earlier, the environment that you are exposed to impacts your thinking, which in turn affects the course of your life. Unless you have been introduced to the world of business ownership or the concept of entrepreneurship, it is highly likely that your mindset is not conducive to running a successful business.

If you want to continue down the conventional path that leads most people towards becoming an employee, then a mindset shift isn't needed. By the time children are in kindergarten, their teacher would have asked them what they wanted to be when they grew up. Children, being products of their environments and what they've been exposed to, often say, "a teacher, a nurse, a police officer, or a fireman." By high school, for Career Day, employees from different companies come to speak to the students to expose them to different career choices, again most commonly as an employee at a company. As students approach their senior year, they are encouraged to think about a career path and/or take a college entrance exam to prepare for college, then choose a major, and then start interviewing for a job before graduating college. Although some students get exposed to entrepreneurship, it is usually through a special program or someone outside of the normal school environment.

Differences in Belief Systems

The belief system that you adopt will either be conducive to succeeding as an entrepreneur or work against it. There are distinct differences between the mentalities of an employee and an entrepreneur. No entrepreneur becomes successful by thinking like an employee. They are mostly contrary to one another. Working for someone else versus working for yourself requires its own unique approach to seeing and doing things.

Your belief system is the foundation of your convictions about what decisions you make in your life and why. For example, I personally believe that entrepreneurship is a calling and not just a vocation. Therefore, I approach it differently than some other entrepreneurs. I see entrepreneurship as a conduit to bringing good in this world, to make a difference, to impact and influence lives with their gifts and talents, and to leave a legacy. To whom much is given, much is required. When you work for yourself, you have the power to create opportunities and jobs for others. And since the majority of wealth in this world is in the hands of entrepreneurs and investors, they have the means to provide solutions to others that can both make money and change lives.

MINDSET EXERCISE 1—Mindset Assessment

Take the following assessment. The purpose is to evaluate the current state of your mindset as it relates to entrepreneurship. There is no right or wrong answer, so your raw honesty is what will get you the best results. Check the answer that more accurately describes you. The instructions for calculating your score are found in the Appendix. Please only refer to the scoring guide **after** you've completed the assessment.

	Yes	No	Points
1. I believe that taking big risks means that I will also lose big.			
2. I prefer to call the shots in the workplace.			
3. I consider myself to be practical and a realist.			
4. I embrace obstacles and see them as challenges to solve problems.			
5. I need comfort and security to thrive in life.			
6. Failure often serves as a motivation for me to get it right the next time.			
7. Work for me is simply a way to pay for my living expenses.			
8. Uncertainty doesn't bother me and feels rather normal.			
9. I prefer to follow a clear career path mapped out for me.			
10. I'd rather create an opportunity for myself that has not yet been defined.			
11. It's exciting to climb the corporate ladder and to be considered for a promotion in my job.			
12. I am known for breaking the rules and setting new norms.			
13. It is best to ask for permission and follow directions.			
14. I feel stifled by structured work environments.			
15. I prefer doing tasks and projects without the pressure of sales quotas.			
16. I live by the mantra, "the more risks, the more rewards."			
17. I thrive best in a team environment where I can play a supportive role.			
18. I am known as a dreamer with big ideas.			
19. Obstacles are barriers that have prevented me from living my dreams.			
20. I forsake my comfort to have success on a regular basis.			
21. Failure has discouraged me to reach my goals on many occasions.			

22. Work is a large part of how I fulfill my life's purpose rather than just a means of provision.			
23. Uncertainty makes me feel very uneasy.			
24. I actively blaze trails for others to follow.			
25. I prefer to have a job description that spells out clearly what my responsibilities are.			
26. I enjoy creating opportunities for others.			
27. Maintaining normalcy is how I like to live.			
28. I'd much rather ask for forgiveness than to ask for permission.			
29. I thrive in an environment that is structured and predictable.			
30. I would enjoy work that directly ties my sales performance to income.			

_____Total points: _____

(See the scoring guide in the Appendix to calculate your score.) How did you score? If you found yourself on the lower end of the scoring scale, this does not rule out your potential to become a successful entrepreneur if it is what you desire to do. It simply means that there is lots of room for you to cultivate your entrepreneurial mindset. That is exactly what this book will do, so keep reading!

Factors That Shape Your Mindset

Because of your environment, experiences, and other influences, your mind is currently programmed for either success or failure. The belief system that you've formed about the 12 fundamental areas that will be explained in this book will determine if you will succeed or fail as an entrepreneur. By examining your mindset towards each of these 12 areas outlined as follows, you will gain an understanding of which areas of your thinking need to be modified. The Mindset Exercises and Assessments throughout this book are designed to help you uncover hindrances to succeeding as an entrepreneur and suggest ways to cultivate an entrepreneurial mindset. These 12 fundamental areas are:

1. Risk—exchanging the possibility of loss for potential gain
2. Leadership—involves setting clear directives, providing oversight, developing talent, and moving the activities of others towards a common objective

3. Vision—having foresight of what is ideal, but is not yet a reality
4. Pioneering/Innovation—discovering what has never been achieved before and succeeding at making it happen
5. Obstacles—anything or anyone that stands in the way of a goal
6. Change—adjusting to a new set of circumstances
7. Failure—an unintended, unfavorable outcome
8. Work—the effort required to achieve success in one's vocation and life's purpose
9. Creativity—the seat of imagination; the ability to create what you saw first in your mind
10. Status Quo—the current state; how things are presently
11. Selling—the process of exchanging goods, services, or intellectual property for payment
12. Self-determination—the intrinsic and relentless willpower to find a way to make things happen

Each of these 12 areas is divided into 12 chapters and carefully explored. To get the most benefit from this book, complete each exercise before proceeding to the next chapter. As you navigate through each chapter, expect to push yourself outside of your comfort zone. The purpose of this book is not to convince anyone to become an entrepreneur, rather, it aims to identify mindsets and thinking patterns that are the most and the least favorable for entrepreneurs, and then provides suggested action items that aid in developing an entrepreneurial mindset.

CHAPTER 1

Mindset on Risk

Risk—Exchanging the Possibility of Loss for Potential Gain

If you plan to become a successful entrepreneur, then consider your comfort zone to be a thing of the past. Nothing forces you to forsake your comfort zone more than taking risks. Taking risks by default goes against human nature because we are creatures of habit and place a high value on what we perceive to be security and stability. In addition, humans prefer predictability and want to feel in control of their outcomes. Entrepreneurship is the antithesis of comfort. It is risky in the sense that there are no guaranteed steady paychecks nor benefits package and there is no one else to blame when things go wrong. Loss of capital and time, hiring the wrong staff, fluctuations in customer demand and revenue, and lots of other external factors in the marketplace are beyond the organization's control.

There is a direct relationship between risks and rewards. In fact, there is a popular saying in the financial investment industry that "the greater the risk, the greater the reward." This is mostly true; however, you can take risks only after you have made an informed decision that is based research and authentic data, a well-thought-out plan, and prior experience. In the words of Warren Buffet regarding experience, "Risk comes from not knowing what you're doing." In addition, after you have taken a risk, you also gain new knowledge, and then the risk from the lack of experience is no longer present. In other words, you have to do something long enough that the risk of failing from not knowing what you're doing goes away.

Risk cannot be totally eliminated, but it can be minimized. Therefore, you might as well make risk-taking your friend. Once you overcome one risk, another one might emerge. On the other side of risk are great possibilities. You will stretch yourself beyond your current capacity, and what you once thought was beyond your reach will suddenly become attainable. As a result, you will become more confident in taking on your next challenge and move to the next level.

On your journey to becoming a successful entrepreneur, taking risks will become the norm over time. With each new risk taken, the trepidation will lessen.

In order to develop the right perception of risk, you must prepare yourself for it by accepting it as an inevitable part of doing business. Taking risks requires you to go against what's normal or easy; therefore, sometimes you need to take a more challenging route that is more likely to produce the results you want. There is just something about taking huge leaps of faith that opens up great possibilities. On the other side of risk is either a big win or an even bigger lesson for you to learn in the event of failure. Either way, both work to your advantage. Think of the old adage, "you'll never know unless you try."

Disappointments, fears, pain, and failures can create mental barriers that dampen our will or desire to try again. They establish a false narrative in our minds that what you attempted was not worth it because the outcome was less than desirable and, in some cases, just downright painful. Perhaps it wasn't your attempt that caused such a terrible result, but maybe it was your inexperience, the wrong timing, the wrong people were involved, or something else was the culprit. None of these mean that you did anything wrong or that you are doomed to get the same set of bad results if you try again under different circumstances.

Reflect back on a time in the past when you wished to be where you are today. Now think about some risks, small or big, that you took to get you here. When you really take some time to contemplate this, you will realize that you've been taking risks all along. Entrepreneurship, by design, will stretch you beyond your current capacity with each new undertaking. When you launch your business you're stretching yourself. When you add a new product or service, you're stretching yourself. If you decide to open a bigger office or expand to another location, you're stretching yourself. Virtually, every decision you make to do something new in your business is a risk. Taking risks will ultimately become just a normal business activity.

One of the biggest risks that I took in my companies was expanding operations throughout Africa. It required me to build a team with people from other countries who followed different customs and were raised in different cultures, and then train them to carry out the vision of my company in their countries. It took a great amount of trust to have my brand represented by people I did not know. I mitigated my risks by properly vetting my new team, getting insights into their cultural differences, and assessing the market. I spent lots of time building relationships with my new team because they would be responsible for leading the charge of offering my company's services in Africa. After almost a year of proper planning and training, I spent three weeks there to launch my services.

The expansion process went relatively smoothly because of the meticulous advance preparation. Was it perfect? No, but I actually learned some things that I implemented when I expanded the company into more countries. Overall, it was very successful and was less risky because I knew what I was doing. I now have a blueprint that I can use when expanding into new markets. I also made so many great personal and professional connections that have enriched my life and business immensely. I would not have otherwise built these new relationships if I had allowed my fears of uncertainty to take over. On the other side of my comfort zone was one of the biggest blessings.

One of the main reasons that people resist taking risks is fear—more specifically, the fear of failure. This is why the brain has to be rewired to focus more on the wins, gains, and successes than the potential losses. Once you have retrained your mind to think this way, your default thinking will shift from "what if it doesn't work?" to "this is going to work!" Remember that comfort zone you've grown accustomed to? Say goodbye to it if you want to be ready for a new level of success and venture down the path of entrepreneurship. As the proverb goes, "nothing ventured, nothing gained."

If you are afraid to speak publicly, for example, the most effective way to overcome the fear is by doing it. Similarly, if you are averse to risk, the best way to overcome your aversion is by taking it head on. Continuing to avoid the risk won't make it go away, nor will it get you any closer to accomplishing your goal. There is a popular acronym for fear, F.E.A.R.—False Evidence Appearing Real. The fear exists only in your mind. Once you have conquered your fears by doing what you were once afraid to do, the fear lessens or is eliminated completely, and it no longer has any power over you.

It will be most helpful to surround yourself with big dreamers and action-takers who will stoke the flames of your dreams and passion. This circle of like-minded people won't feed into your fears, rather, they will encourage you to move forward. If you don't yet have this type of support system, then it is better to minimize or avoid sharing your entrepreneurial dreams until you connect with such people. Those who don't share or appreciate your enthusiasm and are perpetual naysayers, I call them dream snatchers because they have a way of snatching the life right out of your dreams! You can only expand your capacity to take risks when you are around others who do the same things or share the same passion as you do, or, at a minimum will support you in your endeavors because they know and appreciate what you do. Be intentional about expanding your network.

In order to have the right mindset on risk, you must first view taking risks as a positive action and not a negative one. You must see it as a necessary part of succeeding as an entrepreneur. Taking risks doesn't mean you will achieve the desired results, but *not* taking risks will certainly guarantee you won't. The beauty of taking risks is that you will achieve what most people won't in life and in business.

The laws of nature are set up in such a way that we reap what we sow. You can only see a return on what you invest. No investment, no return. You can wish for an apple tree, talk about it, and read up on how to plant and grow one. However, until you take the action to prepare and fertilize the soil, plant the seed, water it, and prune it, you will never get to see the tree or enjoy its fruits. This concept is also true in business. You may have a novel business idea. You spend time studying and learning more about it and even discuss it time and again, but if you don't take the actions necessary to make your business idea a reality, it will never materialize. You must take the leap into the unknown if you want to realize your dreams.

COMPANY EXAMPLE: Dropbox

Dropbox cofounder, Drew Houston, took two big risks that led to two big payoffs. The first was when he was still a college student, he decided to show up unannounced at a startup hub that funded early-stage startups. He was turned away, but instead of quitting, he went on a mission to find a cofounder and then later returned to properly apply and received the startup funding. The second risk was when Houston refused an offer that Apple cofounder Steve Jobs made to acquire Dropbox while it was still in its startup stage. Many startups would have jumped at the chance to be acquired by Apple, but the risk of deciding not to sell has led to Dropbox now becoming a $10+ billion company with over 500 million subscribers. (Olson)

MINDSET EXERCISE 1.1—Mindset Risk Analysis

The Mindset Risk Analysis is designed to help you examine the actual risks you would need to take to realize the rewards you would like to see in your business. You will also be able determine real action steps that you can take to minimize losses or failures which could potentially happen as a result of taking the risk, which is also known as risk mitigation.

Fill in the chart in the following exercise. In the left column, make a list of the risks you must take to launch or advance your business. In the middle column, list actions that you can take to mitigate or reduce your risks. In the right column, list the potential reward you might gain as a result of taking that risk. An example has been provided for you.

(continued)

Risks	Actions to Mitigate Risks	Potential Reward/Gain
Example: The exposure to financial losses by reducing work hours at my job to operate my business full time	*- Save 6–12 months of income* *- Cut all unnecessary spending for 6–12 months* *- Downsize living accommodations* *- Reinvest all profits back into the company*	*- Faster growth of sales in business* *- Greater personal fulfillment*

Questions to ponder: What new information did this exercise reveal to you about your ability or willingness to take on risks? Did you discover from your "Mitigating Risks" answers that you have more control over the outcome from the risks than you realized? Did your "Potential Rewards/Gains" outweigh any perceived losses you had in your mind? If you said yes to both, then you are on the right track toward thinking like an entrepreneur! If you found it challenging to come up with practical ways you could mitigate your risks, don't worry; there is room for growth.

This is an exercise that I would encourage you to take each time you need to weigh the risk against potential rewards. Note, I did not ask you to weigh the risk against potential losses. If you do everything that you can to minimize your losses, then your focus should be on doing what's necessary to get the potential gains. Winners don't focus on losing. This doesn't mean that you shouldn't estimate the costs before launching something new. It simply means that once you do, it's time to focus on the most effective ways of getting the results you want.

Another way to look at risk is the willingness to give up something in hopes of gaining something more. *More questions to ponder:* Would you be willing to give up predictability for the ownership of your time and schedule? Could you forsake a regular social life or leisure and dedicate yourself to spending more time on building a successful business? Are you prepared to give up a steady paycheck to remove the income ceiling on your salary? What are you willing to do to remove the thing that's standing between you and the dream life or business that you want? These are great questions to ask yourself and reflect upon as you evaluate what's really important to you.

Success requires that you expose yourself to the unknown, right in the middle where the risks occur. Risk-takers often achieve success beyond their imagination because they are willing to do things that others won't do. This is a major reason that there are more employees than employers in this world. If you want what you've never had, you have to do what you've never done. There's no getting around this principle. You are going to keep getting the same results if you continue doing the same things; expecting anything different is the classic definition of insanity. Risk is risk simply because you're doing something new and discovering what will work and what won't. In order to overcome risk, you simply have to take it on. Do it. Be afraid if you have to, but do it anyway.

CHAPTER 2

Mindset on Leadership

Leadership—Involves Setting Clear Directives, Providing Oversight, Developing Talent, and Guiding the Activities of Others toward a Common Objective

There are some stark differences between how an entrepreneur and an employee think. One of those differences is on the matter of leading versus following. A follower awaits instructions. A leader takes initiative. A follower relies on the guidance of his/her superiors. A leader is guided by the vision and objectives set for the company. Followers depend on others to get opportunities. Leaders create opportunities for others. A follower doesn't mind being in a supportive role and is just fine to not "call the shots." A leader is effective when making decisions on behalf of others. It takes a guiding set of beliefs to shape the thinking of a leader.

An entrepreneur is a leader who wears many hats. He/she is at the helm of a company, leads a specific group of people, performs autonomous tasks, and provides direction, guidance, and delegation. It is impossible to be an entrepreneur without being a leader. As such, a great entrepreneur must think like a leader in order to be successful.

There are different types of entrepreneurs. There are solopreneurs, serial entrepreneurs, franchise owners, online marketers, freelancers, business moguls, and conglomerate visionaries to name a few. Regardless of the numerous types of entrepreneurs, all of them share virtually the same characteristics. Here are 10 foundational characteristics of a leader:

Has Followers

Without followers to influence, there is no leader. As an entrepreneur, the measure of your impact is demonstrated by how well you compel people to buy from your company, how you shape others' thinking, how you inspire others to be their best selves, or even by how you draw others (employees, stakeholders, loyal customers, partners, etc.) to join you in advancing your vision in some capacity. People follow a leader who has a captivating vision and can convince them that they need what he/she is offering. You don't have to be a social media sensation or even have a massive public following to be a leader, all you need is some followers to influence in some way.

You have responsibilities to your followers. For your customers, you are responsible for delivering on your promise to provide the product or service to their satisfaction. For your employees or staff, it is your job to ensure that they are given a clear vision of where the company is going, its core values, the expectations of their jobs, an environment that allows them to carry out these expectations, and any other promised benefits. If you have investors or shareholders, you will have to honor your commitments to them as well. This is what leaders do.

Gives Instructions

Your staff are also followers who have joined forces with you to help your vision come to pass. It is important for entrepreneurs to provide the necessary leadership and clear instructions for what is needed from your followers to help you fulfill your vision and to reach the goals and objectives that you set. Once you have hired the right staff to accomplish certain tasks, you are then responsible for ensuring that they understand exactly what is expected of them. Until you scale large enough to hand over some of the reigns to other capable people, you will have to take on most of these duties. Entrepreneurs are leading the charge and must set the course by giving directions.

Have you ever been assigned a task with no instructions? It's like trying to assemble furniture with no guide. Imagine the frustration of having the responsibility to do something but no one has made it clear to you how to do it. If you leave room for those who are under your leadership to just figure things out on their own, you are liable for any disastrous outcomes, not them. It also wastes time, increases the chance of mistakes, and reduces efficiency when the team has to attempt to teach themselves.

Develops the Talents of Staff

It is vital to properly train and develop the talent within your company so that you can begin to transition certain responsibilities into capable hands as you scale your organization. Hiring a trainer will be necessary as the business expands, but the business owner must still be involved in conveying the brand message and culture to the trainer to create consistency throughout the organization. The successful entrepreneur will approach leadership from the perspective of empowering those who follow to excel in their roles. Therefore, leaders must be very secure in themselves to recognize when an employee has knowledge or a skill set that exceeds his/her own. A leader cannot be excellent in everything, and so it is wise to hire those who are more competent than you are in some areas. Hiring those who are highly skilled is for the betterment of the company as a whole. There is no room for ego as a leader.

If you develop the skill set of your staff, you expand their capacity to perform better in their jobs. As the staff develop, they can contribute to the growth and development of the company. Investing in your company's talent is also an investment in the company. The longer you retain your talent, the greater the return on your investment. Studies show that training and development is an effective employee retention tool. Employees feel valued when companies invest in their growth. It shows that the company is committed to both the growth of the company and its talent.

Assumes Responsibility for Outcomes

Great leaders understand that they are accountable for all results—both good and bad. Shirking responsibilities is a character flaw. The familiar phrase *"heavy is the head that wears the crown"* is derived from this concept. The burden can be quite heavy at times. Poor leaders absolve themselves of their responsibilities when there are losses and take the glory for the wins. Even with a team of great leaders, the buck stops with the one who is at the top.

If things fail or don't go as planned, the head person in charge should assess where the breakdown happened and take the required action to prevent a repeat of the failure. Conversely, when things go well and according to plan, leaders should keep the company on course so that the success can continue. The price of leadership is that even if you have a poor team that makes bad decisions, you are still to blame. You also get to relish in the victories when the company meets or exceeds its goals.

Exemplifies Behaviors Expected

The best form of leadership is leading by example. The *"do as I say and not as I do"* method of leadership produces followers who lack integrity because it is not practiced at the top. This will set a negative tone for the entire culture of the company. Integrity is when your actions align with your words. If you want your team to show up for meetings on time, you must be on time. If you want them to be excellent in their quality of work, then you must be excellent also. Another great old adage, *"actions speak louder than words,"* is fitting here. You will set the standard for your team by your actions.

In many ways, your company will be a reflection of who you are. Whether they want to be or not, entrepreneurs are role models for their team. Your team will look up to you as someone to emulate. How you handle problem-solving, how you treat others within your company, and many other actions that you demonstrate are teaching others which attitudes and behaviors that are acceptable and which ones are not. This requires leaders to have a reasonable degree of emotional intelligence to understand how their actions and words affect their team.

Makes Difficult Decisions for the Greater Good of All

Having the courage to take charge even in the face of challenges is another mark of a true leader. Staff and stakeholders ultimately look to the business owner for solutions or guidance during a crisis. If sales are down, staff morale is low, your top client is threatening to take their business elsewhere, or your company receives bad publicity, you, as the leader, must step up amid trouble to avert a crisis. Especially in cases where there is much to lose, it is vitally important to demonstrate strong leadership. In a crisis, it may not be wise to put the fate of your business in the hands of someone else.

Another mark of a great leader is being a pillar of strength and resolve, particularly when the company is facing challenges. With a solid team advising you, decision making becomes a lot less burdensome. Some business owners have to decide whether or not to discontinue a product or service, letting go of team members, or developing policies to handle difficult or unsatisfied customers. Although some decisions might be tough to make, their impact on others on the short and long term should be taken into consideration.

Motivates Others to Take Action

As a leader, you have to possess the ability to rally the troops. When there is a mission to be accomplished, it is the leader's job to understand how to best motivate their team. Some examples are setting monetary incentives such as bonuses, honoring them with public recognition, sharing positive feedback, and simple gestures like saying "thank you." If you are unsure about what will inspire your team toward taking the actions you want, then simply ask them. Keeping a motivated staff is a small price to pay in exchange for getting them to accomplish company objectives on a consistent basis. A motivated staff will make your job as a business owner much less taxing.

A compelling vision can also activate your team to do their best. People like to feel like they are contributing to something great. If an entrepreneur is willing to help align the team members' talents, skills, and passion with the mission of the company, very little motivation will be needed to keep them inspired. Passion and purpose are closely intertwined and where you find one you will find the other.

Manages the Strategic Direction

In the context of entrepreneurship, leaders also create the mission and vision of their companies (why they exist and what they set out to accomplish), establish the company's culture, decide the company's brand identity, and provide direction for the company. The leadership responsibilities of an entrepreneur are to identify the short- and long-term goals of the organization and map out a strategic action plan to achieve those goals. This requires a leader to see what's ahead before anyone else can see it and make adjustments accordingly. In order to manage the strategic direction of the company, the business owner must understand industry trends and other external factors that may affect business operations, such as laws, economic conditions, supply and demand, and more.

Leading the way in a business requires having enough foresight to maneuver from one goal to the next in a planned and prudent manner. Business owners must be willing to look ahead in order to be competitive in the marketplace. Setting new trends and staying on the cutting edge of industry changes is vital to staying relevant and in demand. Based on what's going on in the marketplace, the onus is on the entrepreneur to set the necessary course of action.

Holds Their Team Accountable

This one is often difficult for new leaders to do. Taking corrective actions, confronting certain negative behaviors, making requirements known, telling staff when they have fallen short of expectations, reprimanding team members when needed, being firm on deadlines, and so on are normal and necessary tasks of leaders. These responsibilities are not for the faint of heart. It might be uncomfortable in the beginning, but leaders must do these things or the organization will lack structure and order.

Accountability holds team members and the business owner responsible for fulfilling their performance obligations to the company. It also demonstrates that there are standards set by the company that must be followed from the top downward. Without accountability, quality can suffer. Lack of accountability is a breeding ground for low standards.

Seeks Feedback for Improvement

Even the greatest leaders have room for improvement. Getting feedback from others around you in your organization will help you to grow as a leader and help you to remove blind spots that prevent you from seeing your own shortcomings. Seeking feedback demonstrates that you respect the opinions of your team. This also shows that you want your team to view feedback as an opportunity to improve, which contributes toward building a healthy organization.

Feedback provides great data for implementing changes necessary for the growth of both the organization and the staff. It is an effective and proactive means of seeking ways that the company can be better. Getting and giving feedback can also spark innovation because team members are invited to be candid with their suggestions to improve. Some of the greatest ideas are generated by the team. If a leader thought enough of them to hire them, then what a waste of talent it would be to not permit them to express their brilliance.

After every major launch of a service or product into a new market, I host a team meeting to debrief. During this meeting we review what went well and what could have gone better. The team is glad to give their input because they feel connected to the vision. For customers, we send out surveys to ask about their experience and provide insight on what we can do better in the future. The results have given us invaluable business intelligence to apply for ongoing improvement.

These 10 foundational characteristics of a leader provide insight into the mindset of an entrepreneur at the helm of an organization and/or team. Ongoing leadership development is paramount for every entrepreneur. It fosters personal and professional growth while serving as a great example for your team to follow. Leadership development can provide new tools to help an entrepreneur become more effective in leading.

There are a variety of leadership styles, and I'm certain that you will find the one that works best for you. My personal philosophy on leadership is probably best described as a servant leader. I feel that not only is my team there to support me and the company's objectives but I am also there to support my team. I have worked for enough bad bosses to know what is good leadership versus poor leadership (see Figure 2.1). Therefore, I have developed a genuine concern for the well-being of my team.

Poor Leadership	Good Leadership
Must appear strong at all times	Shows some vulnerability and dependency on the team
Points out mistakes and shortcomings of team members	Offers training to team to strengthen weaknesses or utilizes more of their strengths
Drives performance	Inspires performance
Gives orders	Provides coaching and support
Believes that his/her way is the best way	Open to ideas and suggestions from the team

Figure 2.1 *What type of leader do you aspire to become?*

I wrote an article on Forbes.com, *"Leading with Love: An Unconventional Approach to Leadership,"* which explains this concept and more of my convictions about being a leader. (Cuellar)

People who have never served anyone or anything make horrible leaders! There is a disconnect between that type of leader and their team because they have never been in their team's shoes. This often creates a lack of empathy of what it takes for the team to do their jobs well. Unrealistic expectations are typical of leaders who have never served. Leadership is not about barking orders to people or giving commands, rather, it is about inspiring and equipping your team to be at their absolute greatest.

COMPANY EXAMPLE: LinkedIn

From 2014 to 2018, LinkedIn's CEO Jeff Weiner has been rated as one of the top 35 American CEOs of large companies with the best leadership. For five consecutive years, he has maintained a 93% or above approval rating among his employees according to a study conducted by Glassdoor. Employees were the happiest about the company's culture, values, compensation, and benefits package. Specific responses on the survey included free food for employees, a positive and fun work environment, effective and competent upper management, transparency of leadership and quick implementation of employees' feedback on suggestions, and the feeling of being treated well overall. (Glassdoor)

Ultimately, you get to decide what type of leader you want to be. However, an autocratic, dictator-style of leadership will likely be the most ineffective way to lead in most business cultures. Low morale and high turnover of staff are associated with this domineering style of leadership. It is a sign of great leadership when employees or team members are effective, productive, and inspired.

CHAPTER 3

Mindset on Vision

Vision—Having Foresight of What Is Ideal but Is Not Yet a Reality

Entrepreneurs are visionaries who often have a remarkable ability to see what others don't see. Their curiosity leads to imagining something that currently does not exist. They are then able to cast this vision to others (employees, business partners, board members, investors, other stakeholders, etc.) to get them on board. The responsibility of the visionary entrepreneur is to articulate to others what he/she envisions so that those connected with the vision can help make it happen. The future of the organization rests heavily on the entrepreneur's vision, as he/she illuminates the path for others to follow.

The mindset of a visionary dwells in the realm of possibilities. There is an element of faith and conviction needed when you aspire to bring to reality something that only exists in your mind. This is why the mind is extremely powerful! Just as your thoughts can lead you to create something as great as a successful business, they can also keep you stuck and hinder your efforts from achieving your potential. Thankfully, with the cultivation of healthy thoughts, the mind can produce great things.

Having clarity of thoughts is vital for a visionary to allow ideas to flow freely. A visionary must always allocate time to be in solitude and to think deeply. This will make room for gaining a fresh perspective and a new approach to moving the business forward. Almost all of my business insights and creative ideas are generated when my mind is still and at peace. I would imagine that it would be quite difficult to have a clear vision with a cluttered mind.

A visionary's mind has clear ideas about what type of organization his/her company should ideally be, where it should be heading in the short and long term, and what the future looks like for the company. These ideals can also include what the company is known for, what it strives to achieve, and the level of quality it wants to deliver to its customers. A company's vision statement is a written statement that reflects what the visionary visualizes the company to be so that those who are part of the company will read it, connect to it, and execute it.

When deciding on a vision and a vision statement for your company, you should ask yourself the following questions. What do I want my company to look like in five or ten years? What are the core values and mission/goals that I want to align with my company's vision? What goals will my company achieve in the future that I would be most proud of? These are questions that will challenge you to create your ideal company. Your vision might slightly change over the long term, but it needs to remain clear and inspirational.

I recall a point in my early stages as a business owner when I struggled with the identity of my company and, therefore, lost sight of what type of company I wanted it to be. This caused me to lose clarity of my branding message, which ultimately forced me to go back to the drawing board. The end result was a new brand with clear service offerings and a consistent brand message to attract the ideal customer that I wanted to serve. Had it not been for this time of uncertainty and frustration, I would not have realized that my company was better as a global brand instead of relegating it to operate exclusively in the United States. It was well worth the efforts to change!

Unfortunately, my company isn't alone in having struggled with an identity crisis that clouded the vision. Remember that time in 2014 when the U.S. Postal Service launched a clothing line? Yep, that's right. The USPS that we rely on for mail delivery and for buying postage stamps once ventured into the fashion industry—very briefly. During a period it was strapped for cash, the USPS launched a clothing line called *Rain Heat & Snow*.

The clothing was intended to be a high-end all-weather apparel line for men featuring t-shirts, hats, coats, jackets, and footwear. (Krupnik)

As you have probably already guessed it, it didn't survive. To go from mail delivery to fashion is too drastic of a business model adjustment for customers to connect to and a clear sign that the USPS temporarily lost its vision.

The lesson here is that from time to time, companies are faced with making adjustments or reinventing themselves for a number of reasons. When making the necessary adjustments, it's vital to not stray too far from the original vision; otherwise, it's like trying to force two separate companies to operate within the same organization. It won't work. It would be better to just launch and brand a completely different company. Virgin Mobile and Virgin Airlines are part of the same conglomerate of companies, but because the vision for each company is so different, they are separate brands as they should be. No one wants to go to a restaurant and see Chinese, Italian, Mexican, and Soul Food cuisines on the same menu! That communicates to customers that the restaurant doesn't specialize in anything and is good at nothing.

The result of a loss of vision is a lack of sight. When an entrepreneur lacks vision, the direction of the company is in jeopardy, and the staff might feel lost or confused on what to do next because they cannot see where they are headed. Customers might also begin to notice the changes and decide to take their business elsewhere. Sometimes, external factors force the visionary entrepreneur to revise the vision. For example, if a technology you are selling suddenly becomes obsolete, you will be forced to change course or risk going under. More will be discussed on innovation in the next chapter.

A visionary is concerned about taking the company from where it is today to where it should be in the future. If an entrepreneur gets too consumed with the day-to-day operations and neglects what lies ahead, it could result in stagnation and, ultimately, the company won't grow to its full potential. Regular attention should be given to ensure that this does not happen. This can be achieved by having annual vision-casting meetings to ensure that the company stays on track in the direction of its vision.

Visionaries can also see potential opportunities in the market. In the mind of a visionary, problems and obstacles can be turned into opportunities. If a company is operating during a time of economic downturn for example, a visionary will likely see the potential to offer a new product or service that would appeal to a certain segment of the market while providing a solution to the perceived problem. Capitalizing on a declining economy for profit might not seem like an obvious time to make money to a person who does not think like a visionary. Some of my greatest income-producing opportunities in my companies were during times of economic recession and high unemployment.

Visionaries can not only foresee potential opportunities but can also see potential problems that lie ahead and take course-corrective measures to either avert a crisis or propose a solution in advance. For example, when the market started to become more saturated with business coaches and strategists, I was able to see that it was becoming more and more challenging to position my business in my target market. Seeing the writing on the wall, I began researching other markets and found a better fit for my company. My company's website analytics tool helped me to find the right customer fit. Rather than just waiting until the customer base dwindled, this action both averted the foreseeable crisis and created a solution way before the problem occurred.

It is not uncommon for an entrepreneur's vision to adjust when new information becomes available. One example could be that through research and data, the company discovers that it has begun to attract an entirely different market segment than was originally targeted. This will force the entrepreneur to make a decision about the direction of the company. Changes will need to be made to retain the customers that it attracts because that is what makes money for the company. Vision is made clearer with information.

If the vision of where you want your company to go is unclear, then you need to expose yourself to new information. Perhaps you need more data, more industry knowledge, or more insights about your customers. Once I realized that my company's website analytics revealed a large amount of followers in certain countries, I adjusted my vision to expand into those markets after conducting a considerable amount of research. It was a revelation of who actually found my brand appealing. Without this knowledge, I might have relegated my company to serving only customers in the United States.

When a leader has no vision, it is like the blind leading the blind. Decisions are made haphazardly because there is no clear path in sight. Being void of vision is taking a gamble on the future of the organization in hopes that it will somehow reach some arbitrary destination. While there is an element of trial and error with any business, operating without a vision exposes the organization and its employees to chaos and confusion.

How an entrepreneur decides to cast a vision for his/her company is as unique as each entrepreneur. Some prefer a more collaborative effort where the input of an advisory board or leadership team is valued and welcomed. Others might decide to follow a more autonomous approach to casting the company's vision or perhaps a blend of the two. Whatever the preference, casting vision should be done and done often.

It is the vision of a company that pushes the company toward its goals. When people have a clear sense of where they are going, they find ways to get there. So, if you want a team to get behind your vision and run with it, it would be wise to write the vision and make it plain. Otherwise, you might feel like you're pushing your team rather than leading them to something.

There are some instances when the visionary of a company is just the brains behind the operation but not the executor of the operations. I once interviewed the founder of a world famous cupcake shop who revealed to me that she had no knowledge whatsoever about baking or cupcakes. She saw an opportunity to bring something innovative to an area where there was no competition and began to assemble a winning team who could help her to turn her vision into reality. She used her professional skills in radio advertising to get the word out about her new cupcake shop and brought on some investors to fund the vision and the rest is history.

In most cases, the visionary is both the talent and the brains behind the operations, although he/she will likely not carry out the vision alone. As I have said in my previous speeches to aspiring and emerging entrepreneur audiences, if you can carry out your vision alone then your vision is too small. In any case, a visionary sees the ending from the beginning but often doesn't know yet of each step that would be required to make it come to pass. Making a vision come to life doesn't always happen the way you envision it in your mind, and that's perfectly normal.

COMPANY EXAMPLE: Alibaba

In 1999, Alibaba's cofounder Jack Ma gathered 17 of his friends in his home to pitch his vision for the company. He was able to identify that Silicon Valley in the United States was the company's competitor rather than the Chinese, and as such, Alibaba.com should be positioned as a global website instead of a Chinese one. He also envisioned that Alibaba's company culture should be one that embodies a strong work ethic that would rival their Silicon Valley competitors. He believed that innovation would be a core value needed to compete with the United States. Although Ma predicted that Alibaba would be an IPO by 2002, it would be another 12 years before that dream became a reality. However, it was well worth the wait since its IPO reached $25 million, the highest in history to date. Today, Alibaba is one of the world's largest online retailers with an estimated value of approximately $352 billion and operates in more than 200 countries and territories. (Bloomberg)

Ma openly shared his vision with key people who had the capacity to help make it come to pass. When I first launched Pursue Your Purpose LLC, I hosted a launch party where I unveiled my new company to almost 60 key people in the community. Some were a part of the media, some were community leaders, and others were champions who I believed would be committed to sharing what I was doing with their networks. However you choose to cast your vision, do so with discretion to help ensure that the intended audience can help you advance.

CHAPTER 4

Mindset on Pioneering and Innovation

Pioneering/Innovation—Discovering What Has Never Been Achieved Before and Succeeding at Making It Happen

Becoming an entrepreneur requires you to be on the cutting edge of your industry or you run the risk of becoming obsolete. Exploring and developing new ideas, concepts, products, services, technology, processes, systems, and, research and development should be ongoing. There's no such thing as having "arrived" as a business owner, and thinking so would stifle the growth of your business. Remember American giants like Blockbuster, MCI, Borders, and TWA? Their inability to keep pace with changing technology and lack of innovation took them down.

Pioneering means taking risks to introduce to the marketplace a business concept, technology, product, service, or idea that was never seen before and blazing the trail for others to follow. Pioneers are pioneers because they study market trends and conduct research to anticipate what people want and need and develop solutions at the right time. The secret to staying on the cutting edge of innovation is the willingness to try new things and improve upon old ways of doing things—consistently. Sometimes it works, and sometimes it doesn't. The electric car manufacturer Tesla is a pioneer of self-driving cars and is currently developing a prototype for flying cars that was only seen in the 1980s animated cartoon movie series, *The Jetsons*. Tesla's founder Elon Musk, once said about innovation, "Failure is an option here. If things are not failing, you are not innovating enough."

Businesses have evolved over time to keep pace with the changing demands of civilization. Depending on the changing supply, demand, and the standard of living, products and services evolve to cater to the changing needs of customers. The three ages of civilization are the Agrarian Age, the Industrial Age, and the Information or Digital Age. Over time, the basic manual tools used in the Agrarian Age had evolved into mass-produced mechanical tools in the Industrial Age that then became the computer-based tools and systems in the Information or Digital Age we live in today. In this digital age, society is driven by technology and lives are dependent on it.

Regarding technology, the most innovative product of the twenty-first century that has revolutionized the way many people live today is the smartphone. It has changed how people across the globe communicate, manage their lives, entertain themselves, and become more productive professionally and personally. Prior to smartphones, we relied on a variety of devices to carry out different functions that we can now execute with just one smartphone. A smartphone can perform the functions of a multitude of devices, including the following:

- Telephone
- Calculator
- Alarm clock
- Wrist watch
- Flashlight
- Computer
- Radio
- GPS device
- Camera
- Compact mirror
- Portable gaming system
- Camcorder
- Portable mp3 player
- Printed books
- E-book reader
- Voice recorder
- Scanner
- Merchant/payment processors
- VCR

- DVD player
- Timer
- Photo album
- Phone book
- Webcam
- TV remote controller, and more

The innovators behind the smartphone technologies obviously saw a trend that compelled them to adapt to the wants and needs of people. The smartphone is still evolving and will undoubtedly replace the dependency on even more devices than the ones listed previously. Many of the items on this list are now obsolete, while the others have experienced a significant drop in market share. Many more will probably become extinct within the next five years.

Cell phone technology relies on other inventions to accomplish all of these tasks, such as Wi-Fi, Bluetooth, software programming, smartphone apps, and so on. Innovative minds, especially those who work in the technology industry, would be wise to take a serious look at creating systems and products that are dependent on smartphone technologies. The smartphones are here to stay, at least until its successor arrives.

Remember these companies: Kodak, Nokia, Xerox, Blockbuster, JCPenny, Blackberry, MySpace, Sears, Polaroid, Motorola, Borders, Palm, Pan Am, Circuit City, Netscape, Atari, Compaq, Hostess, and AOL? They are all now buried in the graveyard of obsolescence or on serious life support due to their failure to innovate. There are other old companies that are still thriving, but they have experienced shortcomings when attempting to invest in the next greatest idea. One example is Apple.

Apple fell short with its $600 QuickTake Camera which had the capacity to store up to only eight photos with a 0.3 megapixel quality. Apple also once tried to enter the gaming console market with the introduction of the Pippin in 1995. It was another huge flop with less than 100,000 units sold worldwide. Innovation does not always work, but it is better to fail at attempting to innovate than to not try at all. As it turned out, Apple survived, and is arguably one of the most renowned and technologically advanced brands today.

Did you know that ESPN, the sports media company, tried its hand in the mobile phone industry? In 2006, it failed to win over customers with its flip phone, which was intended to provide sports information to its cell phone subscribers. It proved to be a bad decision. Fast food giant

McDonald's is also not exempt from ingenuity going wrong. When you think of McDonald's you think of hamburgers, right? Apparently, the rest of the world does also, as was proven when customers rejected McDonald's' Mighty Wings chicken. Both ESPN and McDonald's are still in business and are undoubtedly still innovating.

There are other products that failed initially but served as a precursor for more successful ones. Although Microsoft's ViewSonic Airpanel Smart Display tanked in 2003, it was a predecessor to the Microsoft Surface line tablets. Microsoft's "smartphones" Kin One and Kin Two were discontinued in just six weeks after hitting the market. They could be considered as the forerunners to the Microsoft Windows smartphones of today. This is just further proof that the Microsoft founder Bill Gates' innovative mindset continues to pervade throughout Microsoft's organizational culture. (CB Insights)

Pioneering and innovation go hand-in-hand. If something does not yet exist, then it means that someone must create it. This is what pioneers do. Pioneers also blaze trails for others. They are not looking for conventional paths to tread. They are not necessarily without fear, but are never paralyzed by it.

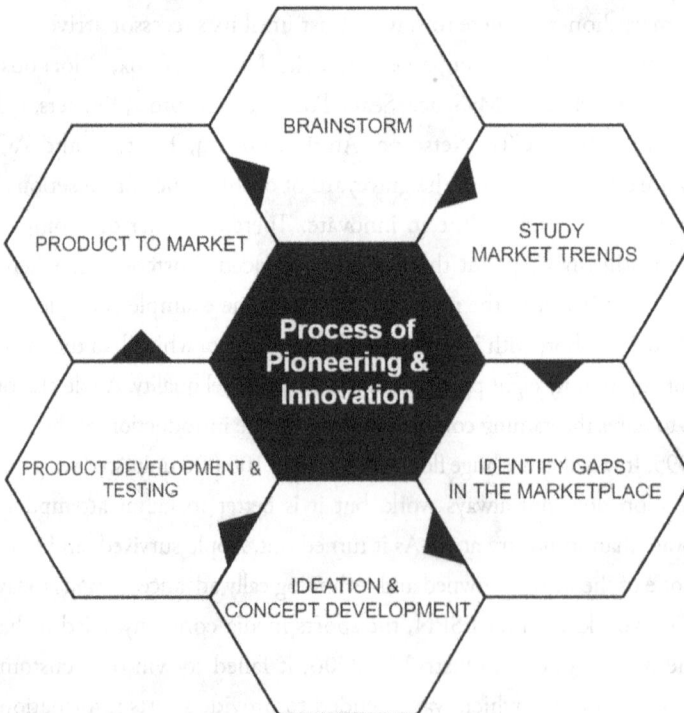

Figure 4.1 *Process of pioneering and innovation*

Pioneers are willing to be on the front lines and lead the way for others—employees, customers, other stakeholders, and the marketplace. The great cost that accompanies pioneering entrepreneurs is that lots of mistakes are made by trial and error since there are no models to emulate. The upside is that they beat other companies to the marketplace by introducing their product or service first, and therefore, have no direct competitors initially. The advantage of not having to share the market with anyone allows them more time to perfect their product or service without any immediate threat from competitors.

I often tell my clients who find themselves struggling to set themselves apart in the marketplace to first discover what other similar companies are doing and then do it differently or better. While this might seem a bit counterintuitive at first, it's actually the very thing that keeps companies on the cutting edge and ahead of the competition. While other companies are scrambling to be seen at the top of the heap in the marketplace, innovative companies veer off and start a new heap. Pioneers, by definition, don't follow the crowd. They are ones who see opportunities before anyone else does, and by the time everyone else catches on, they are onto blazing new trails.

This is how an entrepreneur must think if the longevity of the organization is the goal. Rather than striving to stand out among the crowd, you must leave the crowd to stand on your own. Instead of creating a seat at the table, you must go and build your own table. I attribute a scarcity mindset to be an enemy to innovation. This type of thinking deceives people into believing that there is a short supply of customers in the world, when, in fact, there are approximately 7.2 billion people on this planet. You can create something that a group of people need somewhere in the world; it is an option that is always available if you aren't too afraid to venture into new markets and other geographical regions. Even within your own country, there is probably plenty of new opportunities to explore.

Blazing trails for others is not a prerequisite to becoming a successful entrepreneur. It is, however, a better way of doing business in comparison to the alternative of avoiding risks and playing it safe. When I first started my coaching and consulting firm, I tried to do what most new business owners do—pattern my business after an existing successful consulting firm. That is not necessarily wrong, but using someone else's blueprint for success will cause you to lose some of your authenticity, uniqueness, and ingenuity.

Emulating a successful company in the beginning stages your business should be like training wheels for a new bike rider. Once you figure out how to do it on your own, you no longer need the training wheels. It is the uniqueness of your brand and the problems that you solve (or needs that you meet) for your customers that make you appealing. You can learn a lot from what other brands are doing, like assessing the gaps that they leave open in the market for you to fill or finding areas of their business that you could improve upon. However, this will have limited usefulness if your target market is different than theirs. So, treat what you learn from other businesses as case studies and market research rather than as a blueprint.

Innovation is intentional. It's very easy to get so caught up in the day-to-day operations of running a business that you forget to make time to plan and develop innovative strategies and activities. I've been in business long enough to recognize the ebbs and flows of my companies' operations, so during a lull, I focus on planning and developing innovative services. I can then take necessary time to focus on incorporating new projects into long-term goals. There were some services I created several years before I ever launched them. Then at the right time, I introduced them to the market.

If you want to be innovative, study your industry. Become an expert in your field. Understand market trends and buying behaviors. Become adept at understanding external factors that either create opportunities or barriers for your business. Develop new products or services even if you don't yet see a need for them. Stay fresh. In the words of Jeff Bezos, the brilliant founder and CEO of Amazon.com, "If you double the number of experiments you do per year you're going to double your inventiveness." It's no surprise that Amazon is the largest retailer on the Internet and has revolutionized the e-commerce industry.

COMPANY EXAMPLE 1: Widgetworks

Founded in 2014, Widgetworks is best known for inventing the Airfish 8, a hybrid between an aircraft and a boat. It was designed to reduce flight accidents. It glides on air and can hover just above water and travels about three times the normal speed of a boat or marine craft. Operating on a small V8 car engine and using unleaded fuel, it boasts of comfort, style, and fuel efficiency. It can travel up to 250 nautical miles without refueling and can be a safer alternative to reach remote islands than a single-engine plane or other conventional aircrafts. It is also known to minimize sea sickness. Widgetworks created the Airfish 8 to be ideal for tourists, transporting cargo, water patrol, and exploring unexploited remote areas. (Ibekwe)

COMPANY EXAMPLE 2: Elide Fire

Elide Fire is the company that invented the Elide Fire Ball, "the world's first self-activating portable fire suppression ball." (Elide Fire Ball NZ) More effective and safer than the conventional fire extinguisher, the Elide Fire Ball can be thrown into a small or starting fire from a distance. It will activate the fire suppressant upon contact with the fire and extinguish the fire. If already placed where a fire has started, it can also self-activate when it comes into contact with the fire; eliminating the need for anyone to be present.

Introducing something new into the marketplace that did not exist previously is what causes these two companies to the stand out from among the crowd. This type of innovation is also positioned to revolutionize the lives of its customers and their respective industries. Who could have ever imagined that?

CHAPTER 5

Mindset on Obstacles

Obstacles—Anything or Anyone That Stands in the Way of a Goal

As stated in an earlier chapter, obstacles are perceived as opportunities in the mind of an entrepreneur. They are opportunities to create new ways of doing things and sometimes force reinvention for the better. Although they can threaten the way your business is going, they do not have the power to completely stop the business unless you allow them. Even if you were somehow forced to shut down operations, it then creates an opportunity to start a whole new enterprise. An entrepreneur is like a river that flows around a huge boulder in its path. It just flows right around it. Like a boulder has no real power over the river, an obstacle has no power over an entrepreneur either.

The problem-solving abilities of an entrepreneur will have to kick into high gear to assess how an obstacle is to be handled. Changing course rather than giving up becomes instinctual for an entrepreneur. There's a bigger motivational force that will drive an entrepreneur to overcome a seemingly insurmountable obstacle. Just like a GPS reroutes you to take another way to your destination if a road is closed, an entrepreneur simply will set out to find another course to continue the journey. If you could really see how many routes there are that will get you to your final destination, you would never get discouraged or be tempted to give up. In business, your vision allows you to see the intended destination. The exact route is not guaranteed because you don't know if there will be necessary detours ahead. So, the best option is to just keep going until you arrive at your destination.

This mindset requires a great deal of mental fortitude, tenacity, resilience, and some faith. During the early stages of my business, a lack of capital to grow was always my greatest obstacle. With no investors, little business credit, and almost no personal savings, I had to learn how to leverage my creativity, steadfastness, and unique strategy-building skills to scale my business beyond the startup phase and expand it into international markets. Rather than allow my obstacles to become an excuse or a deterrent, I chose to make another way. I relied on my faith and the vision I had for my life and business to sustain me on my journey and decided to bootstrap my business's growth.

I got the revelation during the early years of running my business that I was not going to allow my bank account balance to prevent me from accomplishing my business goals. As it turned out, that was one of the best decisions I've made because my vision and dreams seemed to always surpass the current cash flow. If I had allowed this obstacle to stop me, I would have shut down my businesses long ago! Instead, I decided to bootstrap my way to success one day at a time. I began focusing on what I had instead of what I didn't. I didn't have a lot of money then, but I had a lot of determination and creativity. I also realized that there is no scarcity of resources or opportunities in this world. I always find what I need or I create it.

I couldn't afford to hire staff initially, so I built a team of volunteers and interns who worked in exchange for job experience. I used free and low-cost software programs to run my business. I worked from home so that I would not incur any unnecessary overhead. I used social media and free press to market my business, and I self-published my first book to market my brand. I reinvested all of my profits into the business for a few years. These are just some of the methods that I utilized to clear the financial hurdles and scale my business. There were many more strategies that I implemented that are still paying off.

Encountering obstacles and setbacks is just a normal part of business and life, and since none of us can escape this reality, we must train our minds to come up with the best ways to defeat them, or they will defeat us. Confronting the things that stand in our path is the best way to deal with them because they will not just go away on their own. Here are some ways to cultivate an entrepreneurial mindset toward handling obstacles.

- Expect they will happen to you at some point, as they do to everyone.
- Don't panic! The best way to overcome obstacles is with a level head.
- Understand that this too shall pass. Nothing lasts forever.
- Take a step back to analyze the situation and look at it from all sides, especially the positive side. It might not be as bad as you think.
- Seek advice and get wise counsel on the strategies you need for your next move.
- Ask your team to pitch in with ideas to overcome obstacles. Some of your best resources are already on your leadership team or advisory board and can help the company push past the obstacle collectively. This is exactly why you should surround yourself with other brilliant people.
- Start making plans for your next steps.

World-renowned media mogul and entrepreneur Oprah Winfrey is a prime example of overcoming obstacles in life and business. She grew up in extreme poverty and was also molested as a young girl. She managed to break through gender and race barriers and became the first Black woman news reporter in her town, but she was ultimately fired because she was allegedly too emotional in her delivery of the news and declared unfit for TV news. She later got her own show, became a billionaire media tycoon, and has been cited as the most influential woman in the world, appearing multiple times on Forbes list of richest and most powerful people. (Oprah Winfrey)

"If you look at what you have in life, you'll always have more. If you look at what you don't have, you'll never have enough," Oprah Winfrey. What Winfrey is describing here is her mindset on obstacles among other things. It is her mindset that causes her to see the glass as half-full rather than half-empty. There will always be some barriers to achieving your business goals. You can choose to allow it to deter you or push you forward.

I can relate to Winfrey in that I also grew up very poor and faced severe challenges that I had to overcome. Challenges definitely make your path a more bumpy road to travel with many unexpected twists and turns.

They are not always easy to navigate, but the effort is worth it. I attribute much of my ability to overcome obstacles to my top 10 tools:

1. Having a positive and healthy image of myself
2. Removing small thinkers from my inner circle and surrounding myself with a strong network
3. Relying on my faith
4. Trusting the process of accomplishing my goals
5. Having a resilient spirit
6. My relentless conviction to fulfill my life's purpose
7. Making a conscious effort to see the positive even in the darkest of moments
8. Self-care with rest and making time to do things that give me joy
9. An understanding that big dreams come with big obstacles
10. The firm belief that my persistence will always pay off

If I can conceive something in my mind, then I just trust that I can somehow bring it to pass. I don't concern myself with the details of how it will happen; instead, I choose to have faith that it will happen. Then I start planning, followed by execution. If you allow yourself to be fixated on the particulars, your goal will start to look more difficult than it really is. Many times I said yes to business opportunities that were challenging even when I initially had no clue how I was going to accomplish them. Thus, I've adopted the motto: "Say yes now and figure out details later."

People whose minds perceive opportunities as obstacles repeatedly miss out on their big break or their moment to do something great, all because the opportunity was disguised as too much work. There's a popular saying that once went viral on social media: POOR = Passed Over Opportunities Repeatedly. This is a true statement. If you are waiting for ideal conditions before you to step out into your next big moment, then life will just pass you by. You'll be watching other people living their dreams while you are sitting on the sidelines waiting for something easy to come along. Rarely do opportunities just fall into someone's lap. Most come by seizing them when they present themselves, regardless of what stands in their way.

COMPANY EXAMPLE: Amazon

Looking at the online retail giant's success today, you would have never guessed that at one point its stock price dropped from $361.88 to a measly $5.81 per share due to the dotcom crash of the early 2000s. Just before the crash, production, logistics, and employee morale suffered. Amazon was understaffed and reportedly resorted to bringing family members on board just to keep up with the demand of orders. Due to some changes in their business model to increase employee morale and to improve logistics, Amazon hired many seasonal workers and made headlines in the news in 2018 with its revolutionary minimum wage increase of $15/hour for all of its employees. This increase was made when the federal minimum wage in the U.S. was set at only $7.25/hour. (Loraine)

Faced with many obstacles, Amazon saw an opportunity to improve its business model rather than folding under the pressure. This is the mark of the mentality that sees obstacles that are disguised as opportunities. This is exactly what is needed to build a sustainable and successful business. Without it, failure is inevitable.

CHAPTER 6

Mindset on Change

Change—Adjusting to a New Set of Circumstances

I stated in the chapter titled "Mindset on Pioneering and Innovation" that entrepreneurs must remain on the cutting edge of their industries and be agile enough to switch gears as internal and external factors arise. Government regulations, customer expectations, new technologies, global economic conditions, and staffing changes are all catalysts of change. Refusal or resistance to change can cause a business owner to lose market share or, even worse, become obsolete. Embrace change. Change forces business owners into new territory that could result in an improvement of products, services, business operations, systems, and processes that they might not have otherwise experienced.

One way to stay open and be ready for change is to commit yourself to becoming a lifelong learner. Listen to fresh ideas from your team, advisory board, or mentors. Attending industry conferences is also an effective way to prevent getting too comfortable. Staying abreast of what's going on in your industry helps to ensure that companies are not behind the innovation curve. One such example of having to be flexible to change at any moment is the healthcare industry. It is heavily regulated and closely monitored by governments, and the introduction of new laws or amendments to existing laws can affect a company's policies and procedures.

People are creatures of habit by nature and will often change only when it is absolutely necessary. Avoiding change inhibits evolving, generation of fresh ideas, and improvement of antiquated methods. Business owners should make it a habit to be proactive in their approach to change. An entrepreneur with an open mind looks for ways to improve by reevaluating current processes, procedures, systems, and technology and makes them part of the standard business practices. A person with a mindset that embraces change will seek out ways be more efficient and more effective in business before they are actually needed.

The willingness to change and adapt not only applies to the business itself, but also to the business owner. Change begins with the change agent—the entrepreneur. If the person steering the ship doesn't turn it, then the ship will continue on the same course. At some point it will crash and get shipwrecked. To become a change agent for your organization, start by being intentional about your personal and professional growth and development. You expand your capacity for change by first expanding yourself. This can be done by reading books, attending conferences, hiring a coach, getting a mentor, joining professional organizations, watching webinars, and networking with people who are smarter than you.

Although you might be ready for change, you have to consider that you may also have to get your team or customers on board with any changes that affect them. Change often affects the entire organization and the people working in it. As such, it is important to establish a culture that makes it as easy as possible to adapt to change. Company communication through team meetings, collaboration apps, newsletters, and emails is necessary to keep your team in the loop and to ensure that staff doesn't feel like the change is happening "to" them rather than "with" them. This type of environment keeps resistance to change at a minimum.

Embracing change is about evolving, growing, developing, and expanding. There are occasions when an entrepreneur has to change the business model of the company. I started my business as a solo business strategist, coaching one-on-one clients who were launching or growing their businesses. As the demand for business grew, I was asked to facilitate corporate training programs, speak at conferences, help establish entrepreneurship centers, and more. I was writing books, doing media interviews, facilitating workshops, traveling internationally, developing new coaching curriculum for universities and other clients, and I soon realized that I had no room in my schedule to accommodate many one-on-one clients.

The demand on my business necessitated a change in the business model. I limited business activities that required the most time with the least reward and also became more exclusive with my services. Had I not done so, I would have lost money trading dollars for hours. My new business model focused instead on more passive income strategies and special long-term projects. I also began delegating more tasks to other team members in order to become more efficient and more effective. If I had resisted making this change, I would have been stuck in the same place with no capacity to grow.

As a lifelong learner myself, I decided to change by expanding my knowledge base and increase both my skill sets and my team's with additional training. This, in turn, helped me to become a more effective business strategist, leader, and entrepreneur. My team also benefited. When you are intentional about your own professional development, you become proactive about making changes. It becomes easier to adapt when change becomes a normal business practice.

Have you ever noticed all of the ongoing updates to your Microsoft Windows operating system, smartphone, and apps? Or how about the constant updates to social media pages like Facebook and Instagram? There is an entire team working behind the scenes at these companies, making changes to stay fresh and to improve the current technology. As annoying as these updates might be, the users eventually adjust to the new and improved way of doing things and ultimately forget the minor inconvenience they endured.

COMPANY EXAMPLE: PayPal

PayPal was founded as Confinity in 1998, and for a short time it was called X.com. It was originally a cryptology company that developed security software for PDA handheld devices. After much debate and some dissention among its founders on whether to stay the course in the cryptology industry or change its business model to focus on transmitting money, the decision was made to change to the business model to an online payment system and rebrand the company as PayPal. Thanks to their ability to be nimble, PayPal not only survived, but has also acquired several other companies for a total combined revenue of over $13 billion and almost 19,000 employees by 2017. (Chargify)

Embracing change is what set PayPal and many other companies on a path of continuous growth. Without change, companies risk becoming complacent, stagnant, and even worse - defunct. The entrepreneur's mindset on change should be to embed it into the company's culture. It is only then that a company can be agile enough to make quick adjustments.

CHAPTER 7

Mindset on Failure

Failure—An Unintended Unfavorable Outcome

In the mindset of an entrepreneur, there is no such thing as permanent failure! Sure, there will be disappointments and setbacks, and things may not go as planned, but none of these can make you and your organization incapable of a comeback. The best way to fail is to learn from it. There are just some things you cannot learn without journeying down the path that leads to disaster or disappointment. In the end, you will have gained a better understanding of what doesn't work, which gets you one step closer to what does work.

Deemed as one of the greatest basketball players of all time, Michael Jordan once couldn't even qualify to play for his varsity high school team. It took Thomas Edison over 1,000 attempts at inventing the light bulb. That means that he failed at least 999 times before finally getting it right! Colonel Sander, founder of the famous Kentucky Fried Chicken franchise, once resorted to sleeping in his car while trying to sell his recipe to various restaurants. After being turned down over 1,000 times, his recipe was finally accepted at the age of 65, which ultimately led to him starting his franchise. Besides having an amazing mindset on failure and obstacles, another great trait that all three of these extraordinary individuals share is self-determination, which will be discussed in detail in Chapter 12.

Let's face it. No one likes to fail. There is nothing enjoyable about it. However, no one is spared from failure. It will visit everyone's business at least once if not multiple times. Along the way, you will pick up lots of nuggets of wisdom that you might not realize are going to help you perform better in your next level in your business. Often times, it may seem like you wasted your efforts and you are staring at the collapse of your business. It can be a real damper on your confidence and, depending on its magnitude, may cause you to feel hopeless. You must be fully convinced that what you learned from your failure can be used as leverage while you move on to the next level in your business. You have to get back up, apply what you've learned, and keep moving forward.

Failure reveals your strengths and weaknesses as an entrepreneur, as a business entity, and also as a person. Being able to recover from a failure develops your resilience, which is required to prevent you from giving up. With every recovery, you will gain renewed confidence that you have what it takes to bounce back in the event of another failure. A new opportunity to succeed awaits on the other side of the failure once you have gotten past it and learned your lessons. The fear of failure begins to dissipate with each rebound.

Failing is often more valuable than succeeding. You will have proved to yourself that you had the courage to try and that fear did not get the best of you. One thing is certain—there is never any success without trying. If you are not failing then your dreams aren't big enough. Accomplishing normal-sized dreams is much easier because they don't require as much time, money, effort, skill, or sacrifice to attain. So if you have ever failed at anything in the past, rather than allow it to stop you from trying again, be proud of yourself for at least making the attempt.

COMPANY EXAMPLE: Nintendo

Nintendo was a giant in the video gaming industry in the 1980s and 1990s and achieved mega success. During this period, it had few competitors in the market. Then came along the Sony PlayStation® and the Microsoft Xbox®. Nintendo struggled to reclaim market share by introducing the GameCube®, which didn't provide the novelty consumers were looking for. Nintendo finally figured out that in order to surpass competition and stay successful, it needed to carve out a niche for itself. That niche was created by the handheld gaming devices called DS® and DS Lite®. Nintendo later made a huge comeback with the Wii®, which was a successful game console that took years to arrive after the failed GameCube®. (Edwards)

Noteworthy Entrepreneurs Who Made a Comeback After Failure

Daymond John—You might know him now as the multimillionaire *Shark Tank* TV star judge and investor, but Daymond John overcame many obstacles to achieve the success that he's known for today. He launched Fubu, a clothing line in 1989 in his early days as an entrepreneur. Struggling to keep his business afloat, John was forced to close Fubu not once, not twice, but three times. He finally found his stride as an investor and the business mogul of The Shark Group. He now has an estimated net worth of $250 million. John is a perfect example of what resilience and hard work can do. (Belanger)

Vera Wang—After failing to realize her dream as an Olympic figure skater, Wang redirected her energy into another passion—the fashion industry. Her dreams were crushed once again after she was passed over for the editor-in-chief position at *Vogue*. Her tenacity finally paid off when she decided to launch her own fashion line of bridal wear and a ready-to-wear department store line. She is a household name in designing wedding gowns, many of them designed for celebrities and public figures. Wang is proof that when one door closes, another one opens. Opportunity can come in different forms if we are patient and refuse to give up on our dreams. (Valentine)

Com Mirza—Although he may not be a household name to many, this CEO of Mirza Holdings runs a reported nine-figure empire with more than 600 employees. Eight failed companies is enough loss and disappointment to make any entrepreneur quit. Mirza instead developed an unshakeable determination.

> Failure teaches you the essential missing parts of the jigsaw to learn to reach real success. When you own your failures and take responsibility, you gain immense power, wisdom, and maturity. Have an open mind, immense intestinal fortitude, and a deep sense of purpose to conquer the struggles, adversity, and obstacles. (Com Mirza)

Failure comes to teach us all valuable lessons that we cannot learn in a textbook, a class, from a parent, a coach, a mentor, or from any other second-hand source. Some failures are tailor-made just for you. Only by experience can this great teacher show us what we are made of. It will test our strength and at times cause temporary disappointment, but its purpose is never to defeat us. I'm here as a witness to tell you that I would have never seen the global expansion of my business had I quit after countless obstacles, mistakes, and failures. Embrace failure when it shows up in your business. Become a student of it and apply all of its lessons during your next attempt. You'll be better off for it.

CHAPTER 8

Mindset on Work

Work—The Effort Required to Achieve Success in One's Vocation and Life's Purpose

Purpose

Purpose, simply stated, is the reason that something exists. Inanimate objects are not the only things that serve a purpose, human beings do, too. When you wake up every day, do you feel like you are doing exactly what you were put on this earth to do? I certainly do, but it wasn't always this way. There is no School of Purpose, unfortunately. The closest thing to it would be life itself. I attribute the discovery of my purpose to my close connection to God.

It was not by accident that I named my coaching and consulting firm, *Pursue Your Purpose LLC*. Once I discovered my purpose, my whole life changed, including my business. Entrepreneurs often have a passion that supersedes working for a paycheck. Their businesses are usually tied to their reason for existing. They have just mastered how to package what they do in a way that can fulfill their soul as well as their bank accounts. Yes, you can profit from your purpose!

If you're going to be an entrepreneur, you might as well do something that you would enjoy doing every day and feeds your happiness. If you haven't figured it out yet, you must know that money alone does not make you happy. Your soul is designed to need more than wealth and material possessions for it to be satisfied. Your work should add to your happiness, otherwise, you'll find yourself trapped in a rat race and just going through the motions. Follow your purpose, and the money will come. You may not get rich, but your soul will prosper, and you can still do very well for yourself financially.

In the mind of an entrepreneur, work is more about carving out your place in the world to fulfill your purpose. Entrepreneurs often align their work with their gifts, passion, skills, and abilities, which also happen to be clues that reveal their life's purpose. Entrepreneurs are often compelled to choose work that is deeply meaningful and purposeful rather than punching a clock and being told what to do. Of course, the end goal is to be profitable, but this is often secondary to their dream. Successful entrepreneurs often sacrifice the financial stability of what a steady paycheck can provide, sometimes for years, to follow their dream. This is proof that it is more about creating their dream life than about instant financial gratification.

Once you discover your purpose, you will learn how to align everything else in your life with it. The type of friends you choose, the person you marry, the type of business you choose, the geographical location you choose to live in, and more will no longer be left to chance. You will become strategic and intentional about fulfilling the reason why you are here on this earth. For me, entrepreneurship is a calling and a divine mission. I won't allow myself to quit when things get tough because I am certain that this is what I'm supposed to do and it is the work that is fulfilling to my soul.

There is a reason that you are drawn to a certain vocation more strongly than others. Your deepest desires and longings, in many cases, will lead you closer to your life's purpose. I started out as a mechanical engineering student in undergrad. I had a full academic scholarship and a great internship making higher-than-average income for a 19 year-old, but there was still something missing.

I just couldn't see myself crunching numbers and calculating statistical variances all day in a cubicle with little interaction with people. I was also disinterested in attending the required classes for a mechanical engineering major. It just didn't suit my personality, and I was unfulfilled and so I struggled. That unfulfillment led me down a path to try to discover my true passion, so I began flipping through my university's course catalogue to find a major with courses that I might enjoy more. It was then that I figured out that business courses piqued my interest. After three business management degrees and running a few of my own businesses, I was right!

I think we do young adults a great disservice in the educational system by not providing better guidance to help them choose a vocation that is more in alignment with who they are meant to be in this world. From my experience with coaching new or aspiring entrepreneurs, I have found that they have already spent years in a career field that had nothing to do with their entrepreneurial ambitions and passions. Many others weren't working jobs that matched their college degree. This shows that college-aged young adults sometimes don't have the capacity to figure out what they want to do for the rest of their lives. In some cases, their desires just changed over time. Either way, the missing link is purpose. Purpose is the glue that ties work and passion together.

If you've ever had to drag yourself out of bed every day after hitting the alarm snooze button a few times, it only indicates that you are not very excited about the work that you do. I've been there! It was super challenging to get to work on time and I knew something had to change, but it took me a while to figure it out. I was trying to force a square peg to fit into a round hole and my dissatisfaction was a clue that what I was doing was an unnatural fit for me. In another job that I had, I was so weary because I felt totally unmotivated to submit the required reports by the deadlines. No one should have to endure this drudgery. Work is not meant to be this way; rather, it should be a gift that we enjoy. We spend so much of our lives working so we might as well enjoy it! Ever since I've aligned my purpose with my work, running my business actually became fulfilling to me on a deeper level.

I have never regretted my decision to change my college major or my career path. It's never too late to change the course of your life if you don't like the direction in which you're heading. However, the longer you wait, the more time you lose that you can never get back. Life is too short to continue traveling down the wrong path. So, change that major, go back to school, acquire a brand new skill set, or whatever you have to do to start over. Your purpose will keep calling you until you answer it. That's why the same dreams and desires often linger in the back of your mind for the past 5, 10, or 20+ years and won't go away.

When you align your purpose with the work that you do in your business, not only is it a gift to you, but you also become a gift to others. As you give of your time and your talents you are actually serving others. This doesn't mean that you should forsake profits. Quite the contrary! It simply means that you should pursue your purpose first because profits won't fulfill you in the long run. Aligning your business vision with your purpose is the easiest way to profit because you are doing something that you were born to do.

COMPANY EXAMPLE: Salesforce

Purpose can also be woven into a company's philosophy of social responsibility and giving back as is demonstrated by Salesforce founders Marc Benioff and Parker Harris. Salesforce started the Salesforce Foundation, which funds millions of dollars in grants, has encouraged 80 percent of its employees to volunteer, and donates or discounts technology to nonprofits in over 110 countries. Social and corporate responsibility is how Salesforce profits with purpose in mind. In this way, business became a vehicle to funnel funding to projects that are in line with the personal core values of the company's founders. (Profit with Purpose)

A company that is purpose-driven gives more meaning to the work than making lots of money does. It gives a sense of purpose while doing good in the world.

If you are struggling to find your purpose, I encourage you to take the following Mindset Exercises. It is a good starting point to uncover overlooked indicators that point to your purpose. For most, discovering their life's purpose is a process that becomes clearer over the course of time. Time will reveal your deepest desires, what you gravitate towards, who you enjoy helping, and your gifts that you put to work with minimal effort.

Purpose is revealed when your passion, gifts and skills, and what you love doing for others intersect. Passion comes naturally. It cannot be manufactured. It's not just an emotion, but it is also a driving force that keeps us motivated to achieve a goal. Without it, interests wane and what you're doing becomes more of a chore rather than enjoyment. Passion could be in the form of love, compassion, anger, frustration, indignation, desperation, and so on. When used for good, your passion serves as a huge part of your 'why' for starting a business.

Your gifts and skills are additional clues that shed light on your purpose. Although they are different from one another, they both work together to make your purpose known. We are all born with gifts. Some may refer to them as talents. We did not work to get them, but we can identify that we have a natural aptitude for something that was just always there. Some people are naturally athletic, or rhythmical, or musical. Others might be more inclined mathematically, scientifically, or technologically.

Skills, on the other hand, are competencies that we have acquired and perfected through training and practice. A skill is something that you can do well because you have taken the time to master it with practice and you've worked to become competent. The main difference is that you cannot acquire a gift, because you were already born with it, but you can develop it and become even more adept at using it. Skills require more effort since you weren't born with a natural aptitude for them, but you do possess the capacity to learn them.

I recommend honing in on your gifts first before you find a skill to develop. That's the shortest path to discover your purpose and do what you love. The added bonus is that you will also have a sense of fulfillment with using your gifts. Birds fly in the sky with ease because that's what they were born to do. Fish swim in the sea with ease, again, because that is what they are supposed to do. Why reinvent the wheel and go against nature when you were already naturally wired to excel at something? Problems arise when you try to alter your natural state to do something that you are not meant to do. There are so many misplaced people in the wrong occupations today. They often choose a vocation based on whatever college majors or jobs that are available rather than choosing a vocation that is based on their purpose. Many may not even have taken the time to reflect on their purpose, let alone make an intentional effort to align their career paths or vocations with it. Once you discover your gifts and your purpose, they can be monetized, packaged, and sold to an audience that you can help or serve in some way. This is what entrepreneurship is all about.

Doing what you love must be a part of the equation when seeking out your purpose. If you don't enjoy doing it then it's not your purpose. One of the greatest disservices that you can do to yourself is to choose a career path, vocation, or business venture based on the amount of money you think it will generate. When people pursue profits over purpose, they end up with full pockets but empty souls.

MINDSET EXERCISE 8.1—Unlocking Clues to Your Purpose, Part 1

In the exercise below, fill in each circle according to the label. Where the circle intersects is where your purpose is revealed. This is the place you'd want to begin when starting a business. You can use the information from this mindset exercise to think of ways that you can create income streams from your purpose.

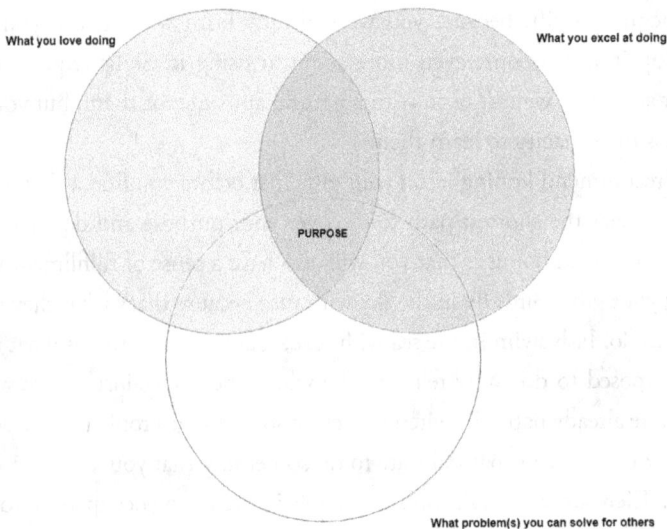

What you love doing   What you excel at doing

PURPOSE

What problem(s) you can solve for others

MINDSET EXERCISE 8.2—Unlocking Clues to Your Purpose, Part 2

This exercise in a continuation of the previous one. It allows you to examine more carefully and to more extensively draw out more in-depth responses. By the end of the exercise, you should have a clearer mental picture of what type of business might be most ideal for you. Answer the following five questions thoughtfully and specifically.

1. What are you most passionate about?

2. What are you naturally good at doing?

3. What problems do you like solving for others?

4. What skills have you mastered?

5. How would you describe your dream business?

Are there any common themes in your answers for questions 1 to 4? If so, you have just unlocked clues to a possible startup. Is your answer for question 5 related to your other answers? If it's completely different, then you will need to work on gaining clarity in aligning your gifts, skill sets, talents, and abilities with your dreams. Your dream business should be something that you enjoy doing for others. If your dream business looks nothing like what you are good at, then you should consider increasing your knowledge and honing your skills to build your dream business, or perhaps you are only the visionary who will hire the right skill set to carry out your vision.

Profiting from your purpose involves a perfect blend of finding a problem that you enjoy solving for others and utilizing your skill sets to do it. Your gifts, talents, skill sets, and abilities can all be monetized. Entrepreneurs get paid to solve problems or meet the needs of others. There is no shortage of problems in this world, and there is one with your name on it waiting for you to solve. In other instances, entrepreneurs provide for their customers' wants rather than their needs or problems. Some cosmetics and gaming electronic devices are not meeting needs, but the beauty and electronic gaming industries are doing great and are not going anywhere anytime soon. Luxury brands are similar in concept, but there is still a large market that aims to fulfill clients' craving for opulence. Whether you choose-needs or wants is up to you.

Legacy

Leaving a legacy is also a part of an entrepreneur's mindset on work. A business is something that can be passed down from generation to generation. A job cannot be inherited, obviously because there is no ownership. As an entrepreneur, you can create income-earning opportunities for heirs and other family members, the community, and others. Business ownership is thought of as a wealth creation vehicle. Most people will not get rich or wealthy by working for someone else all of their lives. Leaving a financial legacy helps to secure the welfare and prosperity of the family who succeed the business.

Making your mark on this world is also a part of your legacy. What do you want to be known for at the end of your life? What would you like to contribute to this world to make it a better place? The world is waiting for what you have to offer. Unfortunately, many people are living beneath their greatness because they are choosing the conventional path of the masses. "Go to school and get a good job," they say. Who is "They" anyway? Follow your instincts to do something greater than what the masses are doing.

Long after I'm gone from this earth, I'd like to leave behind something that is still making an impact and still producing income for my family members. Businesses, books, articles, other published works, intellectual property, and inventions are all legacy-building tools. Just think if all 7+ billion of humanity carefully considered how we could all leave this world a better place after we have departed. I consider it my duty, not only as an entrepreneur but also as a human being.

Self-sufficiency

Work to an entrepreneur is a form of establishing independence from the fluctuating conditions of the job market. In fact, some former employees who were laid off, underpaid, demoted, or had their jobs eliminated found their entrepreneurial spirit by circumstance. While the unemployment rate varies by country, one thing that remains the same is that, if the jobs don't exist, then the people themselves must create them. There is an element of freedom that entrepreneurs get to enjoy because they are not at risk of losing their jobs due to circumstances beyond their control, and, to a large degree, they control their own destinies, professionally speaking.

There is also the possibility of having multiple streams of income to help recession-proof your business, which I highly recommend.

During my last few years of working in Corporate America full time in the financial services industry, the market crashed in 2008 and the United States went into a recession. Many of my colleagues were laid off during not one, not two, but THREE rounds of layoffs within a period of one year. The stress of the uncertainty of being on the chopping block next, along with some other factors, caused me to rethink my whole career. I ultimately made the decision to resign on June 26, 2009 and never looked back. I had operated side-businesses for several years previously, but this time I was ready to operate my business full time.

Companies can demote or fire employees at will, reduce benefits packages, cut hours, and there is virtually nothing that can be done about it. Even the federal government can shut down and withhold pay indefinitely from employees as has happened in the United States. If a company folds then employees are out of their jobs. There's a whole host of other dire situations in which employees can find themselves in simply because they are at the mercy of management decisions. Entrepreneurs typically prefer to be independent and self-reliant in order to sustain themselves.

Personally, I would feel more uncomfortable with having a company control too many aspects of my life than with the uncertainty that entrepreneurship creates, including the absence of perceived safety nets like a salary and a benefits package. I would gladly trade these in exchange for depending on my own talents to live and work on my own terms. It's not always easy, but I value my independence. It is a large part of what I enjoy most about running my own businesses.

While it is important to highlight all of the benefits of being your own boss, the reality is that being self-sufficient comes with an enormous responsibility. You must be disciplined in how you manage your time. With entrepreneurs especially, if you don't work, you don't eat. Your mindset must be focused on maximizing your time, or you will squander this great resource that you have at your disposal. There is no one for you to rely on to manage your time. Only you can do that.

Self-sufficiency and legacy were important to me, but so was the lifestyle I dreamed of creating for myself. I wanted to be able to have enough time and money to travel when I wanted to and to do work that was more meaningful to me. And today, my businesses and my life look much like I envisioned it to be several years ago. One of the goals that I set for myself was to be able to live a location-independent life, meaning that I would be able to do my work from anywhere. This is a reality for me today. What type of lifestyle do you envision creating with your business?

Lifestyle

If you prefer to design your work around your life instead of the other way around, entrepreneurship will probably be a better fit for you than working a conventional 9-to-5 job. Very few career paths allow you to set your own schedule, determine when and for how long you'd like to take a vacation, or when you can get a pay increase. As an entrepreneur, you can decide all three and more.

There is a growing segment of entrepreneurs who refer to themselves as digital nomads. While a small number of them work as remote employees of companies from virtually any location that has an internet connection, the vast majority are self-employed freelancers or business owners who created a location-independent life for themselves. The trend towards remote work indicates that more employers are recognizing the need to create flexible work arrangements for those who are more autonomous and like the flexibility and freedom of working from home or from anywhere in the world. A positive outcome of this arrangement is the benefit of lower overhead costs for employees. The more remote employees there are, the less need there will be for larger office spaces with higher rents, office furniture, higher utility costs, and so on.

This trend also reveals that technology has removed geographical borders for people to conduct business. With a laptop, a strong internet connection, VoIP or video conferencing apps, and the right productivity software programs and apps, a business can exist without even having a physical location and without being physically present. Entrepreneurs are taking advantage of these new conveniences and are integrating them into the lifestyle they want. I certainly did.

I am at my best self when I'm travelling, speaking, coaching, consulting, lecturing, and writing. In fact, I wrote a large portion of this book while at a peaceful condo nestled in the woods with a view of a pond, in front of a cozy fireplace. The work that I've created for myself in my companies allows me to travel to new and exciting places throughout the world. This is how I create the lifestyle that I want on my terms while getting paid to help thousands of people each year. I call these 'The Four Fs' of the entrepreneurship lifestyle—Freedom, Flexibility, Fulfillment, and Finances. Freedom gives you the independence to create the kind of business you want. Flexibility affords you the ability to live without others putting restrictions on your time. Fulfillment allows you to align your work with what gives you joy and a sense of purpose. Finances have no salary cap when you work for yourself because you have over control how much you sell and for how much.

CHAPTER 9

Mindset on Creativity

Creativity—The Seat of the Imagination; The Ability to Create What You Saw First in Your Mind

Creativity to the entrepreneur is like water to a fish. It is necessary for survival. Entrepreneurs create businesses from a mere idea that once existed only in the mind. Taking an idea from concept to market requires the ability to imagine. Creativity is activated each time an entrepreneur thinks of ways to invent a new product or service, improve upon an existing one, or to solve a complex problem.

Creativity is also useful when you have less resources than what you need to make your business goals come to pass. When I coach emerging entrepreneurs, I always tell them that it is their creativity that can make up for what they lack in terms of resources, including money. This is a truth that I've applied in my business many times. Never underestimate the power of your creativity. It is in your nature to create and make something out of nothing and to make something that's already great even better. This is why it is imperative that an entrepreneur is intentional about nurturing his/her creativity. Creativity is the birthplace of new ideas.

If you can imagine it, chances are that you can do it. Not every thought is worth bringing to life, but many of them are. Have you ever gotten a fleeting thought of some new invention that would be cool if it existed, but never acted on it? Or, maybe you've thought of a technology or a cool device that would make people's lives better. These are moments of creativity that you might have underestimated as just another random idea. Your life could drastically change if you just took the time to nurture the random creative thoughts you get. You might just be missing out on a million dollar deal!

If you are struggling with getting creative ideas to flow, consider the following questions:

- What information, product, or service do you wish you had to make your life or someone else's life better?
- What technology that doesn't currently exist would make life, work, or business easier?
- What processes do you feel that you could improve upon?
- What do customers frequently complain about on companies' social media pages?
- What product or service offering could you pitch to an existing company and perhaps partner with them or contract out your services?
- What issues do you often notice other people around you are struggling with?
- What social problem in this world bothers you or angers you that you wish you could solve?
- What recurring problems show up in media headlines?

Be thoughtful in your responses. They will reveal solutions that are probably needed for a group of people. These group of people are your target market who can then become your customers. These customers will then pay you. This is how simple starting a business can be. You don't need a 30-page business plan and investor pitch deck or a million dollars in startup capital. Just start with a good idea.

I use the Memo app on my cell phone every time a new idea comes to mind, even if it's 3:00 a.m. I have enough book titles to last me a lifetime! Some ideas I act on very quickly to prevent the opportunity from passing me by. In my downtime, I find time to create new product ideas, new services, new ideas for marketing campaigns to discuss with my team, and much more. Everyone is creative, but not everyone is in an environment that is conducive to birthing new ideas. Surrounding yourself with the right people, places, and things will inspire you to do so.

COMPANY EXAMPLE: Volition Beauty

Launched in 2016, Volition Beauty has a very creative business approach. It uses a crowdsourcing-type business model to source the latest and greatest beauty inventions from ordinary people. By tapping into the public to submit their own beauty creations, the company capitalizes on untapped talent and gives them a platform to test and sell their products to the Volition Beauty community of 300,000+ followers.

"So, you submit your idea, then we partner you with a top lab. Once we get to a prototype, which the innovator is very, very involved in approving as we go through iterations of that, then, it goes up to campaign on our website. But we don't only use the [website] campaign. We also use our social channels to get the word out, and we expect the innovator to help get the word out with her community, friends and family. We've had innovators talk to their local press and be like, 'Hey, I'm sending an idea to Volition, and it's up for campaign.' I think the press love those [stories], and we've had nothing to do with it," states Patricia Santos. (founder, Beauty Independent)

IDEATION PROCESS

1 Who?
- Geographic region
- Ethnic group
- Gender group
- Age group
- Socioeconomic

2 What?
- App/Software
- Intellectual property
- Product
- Service

3 When?
- Start to finish timeline
- Launch date

4 Where?
- Geographic location
- Online
- Physical building/office space
- Retail stores

5 How?
- Subscription model
- Trade shows
- Amazon.com/Alibaba.com
- Celebrity endorsement/social media influencers
- Online marketing campaigns

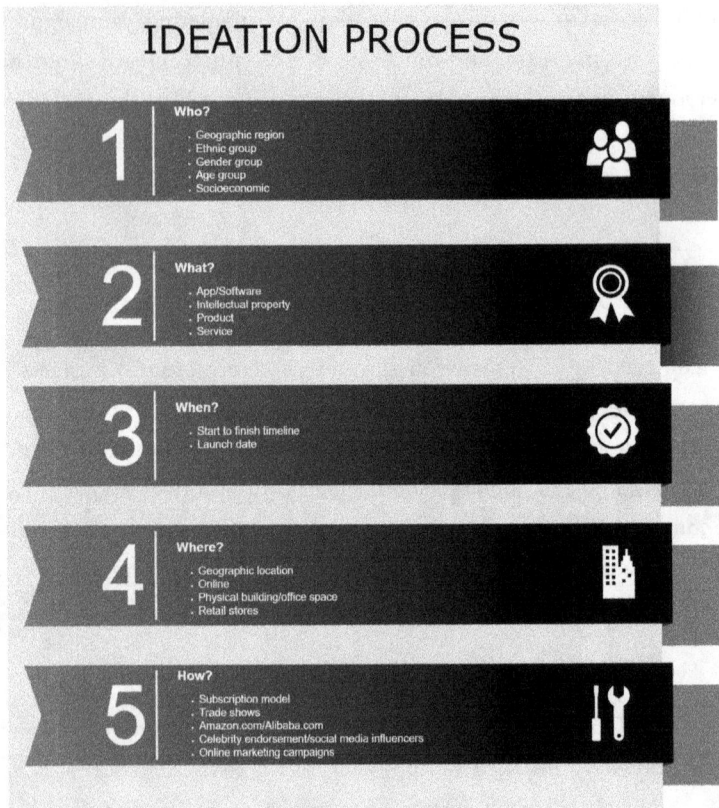

Figure 9.1 Ideation Process

For whom are you creating your idea (product, service, etc.)? Answering this question will reveal your intended audience, demographic, or target market for which you are creating. *What* type of concept, solution, service, or product is it? Is it an app, a prototype for a new invention, or an implementable process that will improve the way people do things? This will specifically define the thing that you are creating. *When* do you plan to have it completed, implemented, or launched into the market? A date or time frame gives context to how long the process will take to get from concept to reality. *Where* do you plan to implement or sell your concept, solution, service, and so on? Think in terms of platforms, geographic locations, online, and specific places. *How* do you plan to implement or sell what you create? Your answers should reveal the process or steps you plan to take to sell or implement your creation.

MINDSET EXERCISE 9.1—The 5 Ws Ideation Process

Ideation is simply the process of coming up with new ideas. It's like brainstorming on steroids because it not only helps with generating ideas but also with organizing them. Both established and emerging entrepreneurs use various ideation techniques to create new products, services, concepts, and processes, and improve upon existing ones. I love simplicity and avoid complicated charts and graphs, so I created the *5 Ws Ideation Process*. This exercise is to the point.

In the following table, fill in the Who, What, When, Where, and Why of the idea that you would like to develop. You can use it to create new products, services, technology, intellectual property, and solutions to problems. In some cases, it will make more sense to complete the "What" first. Use the order that works best for you. An example has been provided for you.

Who?	What?	When?	Where?	How?
> Executive MBA and senior-level business students > Emerging and existing business leaders > Aspiring and emerging entrepreneurs > Emerging thought leaders	*Cultivating an Entrepreneurial Mindset* book	1st quarter of 2019 and beyond	Worldwide at universities, business schools, university libraries, public libraries, business conferences and workshops, online book distributors, book signing events, author showcases, and book clubs	Research and hire a book publishing company to publish, market, and distribute the book

I would also encourage you to open your eyes and be intentional about seeing what problems exist in the world for which you could come up with creative solutions to help lots of people, and then cash in on them. When I travel, I tend to see more opportunities than at any other time. It's just one more reason that I love to travel. I see more solutions to problems than I have time to entertain. Try out different environments to see what makes your creativity come alive. Get away from your daily routines and habits and go somewhere different. You might discover that being near water, a fireplace, overlooking a particular scenery, listening to certain music, hanging out in a coffee shop, or just having brainstorming sessions with other likeminded people spark your ingenuity.

When you are intentional about doing something with the ideas that come to you, you are making room for your creativity. This will expand your capacity to receive more and more ideas. Start by writing them down or using a memo or voice notes app to record them. Then begin to implement the ideas that seem to fit into your life right now. Which ideas do you have the capacity to act on today? Don't worry that you don't have all of the people you need or the financial capital to get things going. Write a plan, start taking small actions toward making your idea a reality, and the rest will follow. You might have the next Hollywood movie script inside of you or the next invention that will revolutionize the way humans cook food. The world is waiting for your idea to come to life. What are you waiting for?

Examining Modern Trends in Entrepreneurship

Whatever creative ideas you generate for your business, modern trends dictate the direction of entrepreneurship and how business is being conducted. You must pay attention to these trends if you want to stay relevant and on the cutting edge of doing business. At the time of the writing of this book, we live in the digital age, also known as the information age. There is a focus on cryptocurrency, which is a form of digital currencies. Artificial intelligence and robotics are also areas where many companies are spending millions of dollars on research and development. Cloud computing has now replaced the need for physical devices such as servers to store digital data.

Blogging has also been a creative way for writers to monetize their skills into a business. With a large enough following, bloggers can become platforms for advertising. Because most TV ads can be skipped on playback with DVR, companies have begun to capitalize on the captive and highly targeted advertising of bloggers' audiences. If you've ever wanted to have your own radio or TV show on a particular topic, a technology like podcasts allow you to self-produce content from the comfort of your own home. You can broadcast it to your audience by video, audio, or both. Once you have reached a certain number of followers, you can attract advertisers who will pay you to promote their brands with your audience.

YouTube influencers with a large number of subscribers are doing the same, in addition to getting paid for doing product reviews on their YouTube channels. Individuals with thousands or millions of followers on Instagram and other social media platforms are getting paid to endorse products and services and have the influence to make videos go viral with just one post. Some YouTube channels do beauty tutorials or offer lifestyle and travel tips and a whole host of other things. Celebrities and entertainers have even jumped on the bandwagon of the social media craze and have gotten their products or music to go viral through the social media accounts of ordinary people.

If you have a deep knowledge or expertise in a particular area, e-courses can be created and sold through sites like Udemy or Kajabi. This is one way to sell intellectual property with no overhead, no employees, and no major active involvement in the business activities. If you are able to market your courses well, this is a viable way of creating an income stream for yourself. You'd just have to think of some information that would take others years to acquire, create an e-course out of it, and then sell it.

Affiliate marketing is a passive income strategy that allows people to earn a commission from an online retailer for directing traffic to its website for sales. It usually involves a trackable link that traces sales that are made when a customer clicks it to make a purchase. The Amazon Associates program is one of the most respected affiliate programs worldwide. If you have a website, you can allow Amazon to advertise its products on your website in exchange for getting paid an advertising fee. It's a relatively easy way to earn money for promoting a company's products and services.

E-commerce is a growing trend that facilitates buying and selling products online. You can buy the products you want to sell, or make them yourself, and then use an online shopping platform like eBay or Etsy to sell them. This replaces the need to restrict selling products to a local physical brick-and-mortar store and opens your business to national and global audiences. If you want to get into the retail business without the hassle of maintaining the inventory yourself, you can use dropshipping to profit from forwarding order details to the supplier who is responsible for shipping the products. In other words, the customer places an order and then you send the order to the wholesaler or another retailer to fulfill without ever touching the product.

What Are Other Entrepreneurs Saying?

More fresh voices in the global entrepreneurship community weighed in with their insight on where they believe entrepreneurship is going in the 2018 Forbes article, 23 Trends That Will Shake the Business World in 2018. (Young Entrepreneur Council)

Here are some of their thoughts on the areas to watch going forward if you want to think like an entrepreneur.

Blockchain—Blockchain is the technology that records cryptocurrency transactions. Entrepreneurs with high-tech skills will want to consider developing a technology that will increase security for blockchain users. The banking industry has already begun to integrate blockchain technology into its business processes, and more and more industries are looking to do the same.

Live video—Digital media is increasingly becoming the norm given the way people consume information globally. Traditional media such as news outlets and magazines like *Forbes* have already begun featuring video segments on its various online "channels." More companies like BuzzFeed are providing a unique form of infotainment to its audience. Facebook and Instagram have a live feature that allows companies to interact with its audience in real time by live video.

Customer contact by text—Once considered spam, a growing segment of customers now welcome text messages as a form of communication. Whether it's an invitation to an exclusive sale, or a notification that your order has been shipped or delivered, texting is no longer considered an unwelcome form of communication between customers and their businesses. The Facebook Messenger app and WhatsApp are currently popular platforms for companies to communicate with their customers.

Chatbots—If you think you or your team must be present at all times just to be at the beck and call of your customers, think again. Chatbots can automatically create tickets to a company's help desk while setting the expectation of response time to your customers or generate automated responses to simple inquiries asked by website visitors. It's another way for you to communicate with current customers and capture the contact details of potential clients.

Coworking arrangements—Both established and emerging companies are using a more collaborative work environment to facilitate teamwork and idea-sharing. The layout of a coworking space is often a concept of an open office space without walls or partitions. Some coworking offices are dedicated for the exclusive use of entrepreneurs, independent contractors, and freelancers. This setup is conducive to networking, synergy, and eliminating the isolation of being a solopreneur. It's also a great money-saving strategy for startups and a great alternative to leasing office space with long-term contracts since many coworking spaces offer membership with flexible terms.

Nontraditional education—With the increasing number of students trying to avoid student loan debt and find the fast track to earning a good living, formal education is not as coveted as it used to be, neither by students nor by employers. There are alternative means of getting education such as through certifications (especially in the tech industry), which are sometimes equally valued, if not more so. With the growing trend of millennials and Generation Z looking at owning their own businesses, obtaining a viable skill set through nontraditional education is becoming a popular choice. Massive open online courses (MOOC) and Coursera are examples of alternatives to traditional education.

More dependency on automation—Automation is the entrepreneur's best friend. Here's a list of business processes that can be automated:

- Directing phone calls
- Some email responses
- Getting signatures on documents
- Initial customer service or IT ticket requests
- E-commerce orders
- Social media posts
- Lead-generation campaigns
- Newsletter subscriptions
- Abandoned shopping cart email reminders
- Appointment scheduling and reminders
- Recurring invoicing and billing
- Payment reminders

There are many more processes that can be automated. Manual processes cost time and money because you need to hire a person to do them. Automation not only saves time and money but it also increases effectiveness (reducing the chance of human errors) and efficiency (productivity).

Marketing segmentation by social media platforms—As different social media platforms emerge, it gives way to the different audiences that exist and how your business might more effectively cater to them. There is very little overlap between Snapchat users and LinkedIn users. For example, 86 percent of Snapchat users are aged 34 and below, whereas 64 percent of LinkedIn users are aged 30 and above. You can partly identify your target market based on which social media platforms they use the most and begin advertising and engaging where appropriate. (Spredfast)

Mobile retail sales—Capturing more sales from customers who frequently use mobile devices should be a normal part of doing business. In 2012, retail sales from mobile devices only comprised about 11 percent of all sales. In 2016, that number jumped up to approximately 48 percent and is still rising. Consumers have access to cell phones and other mobile devices like never before, and this is likely not going anywhere anytime soon. Running web ads is simply a smart way to capture new business.

Focusing on diversity—Increasingly, companies are seeing the value of promoting gender and ethnic diversity within the organization and giving such diverse groups a fair and equal representation. As such, entrepreneurs who do not view diversity as a core value may risk appearing insensitive and alienating an entire segment of customers. Diversity is viewed as an element of your company's social consciousness by potential customers and other stakeholders.

Have these ideals shaped the way you perceive entrepreneurship? The days of conventional offices with cubicles where employees only interact with customers by phone or email are slowly becoming a thing of the past. If you are thinking of going into today's business climate expecting the traditional work arrangements as your parents or grandparents did, you will have to do a mental paradigm shift to embrace what I call *neo-entrepreneurship*.

Examples of Creative Business Models

Once you have completed the ideation process and come up with what you want to sell and to whom, you will need to decide on a profitable business model to operate your business. According to John Mullins, author of *Customer-Funded Business*, there are at least five business models that you should consider to circumvent startup or early-stage funding challenges. Four of them are explained below.

1. *Matchmaker model*—Business platforms that bring buyers and sellers together are using the matchmaker model. These companies are not in the business of selling the products or services of others themselves, but act only as an intermediary and use their websites as meeting places or a marketplaces where transactions can occur. One example is Travelocity, which connects travelers to airlines, car rental companies, cruise lines, and hotels. Travelocity collects a fee for each transaction that is made. It is responsible for providing the technology and some customer support.

2. *Pay-in-advance model*—Requiring payment upfront works well for some types of businesses. Some medical service providers require a copayment. Consulting, home remodeling, or construction projects may require a deposit to secure booking or to purchase materials.

It is not unusual for service shops such as clothing alterations or shoe repair businesses to charge their entire free upfront.

3. *Subscription model*—Memberships, premade meal delivery, e-courses, beauty products, offering a discount for automated on-going customer billing, digital streaming, massages, and many other products or services can be sold on a subscription basis. If customers purchase something on an ongoing basis, whether weekly, monthly, quarterly, or annually, it can most likely be sold as a subscription. Some examples include Amazon Prime, Netflix digital streaming, and McBride Sisters Collection wine club.

4. *Scarcity model*—Have you ever noticed the companies that use ads that claim that quantities are always limited or offers are only available for a limited time? Then you have just observed an example of a business that uses a scarcity model. Other examples of this are flash sales. These are companies that thrive on turning over products at a rapid pace, and, more likely than not, they have made a deal to pay the supplier only after the products have sold.

Based on the above list, you can choose one business model, combine business models, or develop an altogether new, unique business model. There is no right or wrong business model, only the one that works best for your company. This is the beauty of creativity. If you can imagine it, then you can achieve it.

CHAPTER 10

Mindset on the Status Quo

Status Quo—The Current State, How Things Are Presently

An entrepreneurial mindset is one that challenges the status quo rather than accepting it. Going along with how things have always been done does not foster success in business; instead, it impedes growth and produces mediocrity. Doing things the way everyone else does won't produce innovation, nor will it disrupt the marketplace by introducing something new. Entrepreneurs have a propensity towards being unconventional because it is a thrill to do something that is out-of-the-box. In the words of Albert Einstein, "Creativity is intelligence having fun." I couldn't agree more. Let your intelligence out to play!

Escaping the status quo of the workplace is often a driving force for aspiring entrepreneurs to leave and start their own businesses. Entrepreneurs who are displaced in a work environment have a difficult time just going along with things and fitting into the mundane environment. Doing things according to the status quo is contrary to what the entrepreneurial journey is all about. Entrepreneurs embrace newness and fresh ideas that inspire them. In fact, they thrive on them. Therefore, entrepreneurship is a better fit for who they are as people. Some innovative companies have learned to embrace employees with an enterprising spirit and foster it. These individuals are commonly referred to as *intrapreneurs*. However, these types of companies are rare outside of places like Silicon Valley.

The status quo stifles the very creativity that entrepreneurs need to imagine, invent, produce new ideas, products or services, and to stay inspired. When companies excel at something, it is often because they have forsaken the status quo. Airbnb, Uber, and Tesla, all go against the grain and have achieved great success as a result. Airbnb challenged the norms set by the hotel industry, which had previously monopolized the short-term accommodations industry. Uber disrupted the taxi industry by using a similar model to Airbnb, and both operate technology-driven business models, except Uber is in the transportation industry. Uber has successfully taken away a large market share from the market once dominated by regular taxis. Tesla released the first self-driving car into the marketplace, a superior driving experience to all other cars on the market.

Doing what most people do will get you what most people get—a traditional 9-to-5 job. This type of normalcy won't help you succeed in running a business, which is why it is vital that you have a paradigm shift in your thinking. This is not to downplay those who choose the workplace as their career path as if it's inferior to do so, but this is about understanding what is necessary to cultivate an entrepreneurial mindset and how to do it. If you prefer to color within the lines, are uncomfortable rocking the boat, or are afraid to break the rules, then entrepreneurship is likely not for you.

If you have been living a conventional life, then it's time to start taking steps toward the edge of your comfort zone and, ultimately, making a life outside of it. For some people, going to dinner or a movie alone is a big step towards leaving their comfort zones. I'm not suggesting that you start bungee jumping or skydiving, but just try something that you've never tried before to broaden your horizons and increase your exposure to new things. Perhaps trying a new dish in a different restaurant in a different part of town will be a good start.

I am an admirer of Sir Richard Branson, the business mogul behind Virgin Airlines, Virgin Records, Virgin Mobile, and more. I have a tremendous amount of respect not only for the conglomerate he has built but also for how he takes on life. Online, I've seen photos of him kite surfing and have read about his attempts to make the 7,000 mile journey across the Atlantic Ocean. (*Business Insider*)

I think there is a connection between being adventurous and being out-of-the-box. My best adventure was traveling to five cities in South Africa, Namibia, and Canada in three weeks, complete with yachting, eating ostrich for the first time, and dancing to tribal African music in front of an audience! This is my way of not only enjoying life but also resisting the mundane. Resisting the mundane helps me to stay fresh and innovative. Too many dull moments in life will make you dull too.

As I reflect on my years in Corporate America, I wonder what my superiors were thinking when I would question the way things were done. I challenged inefficient processes and suggested improvements, but it seemed to have fallen on deaf ears. The company culture was set to embrace the status quo. It's frustrating for someone with an entrepreneurial spirit to just go along with things simply because that's just the way it is. That was one of the first signs that I was not cut out to be an employee for the rest of my career.

I recall telling my manager at that same company during a performance review session that she was underutilizing the talent in our department. I alluded to the differences between managing and leading. Some nerve I had! My intention was not to be disrespectful, but I saw some things that either she didn't see or didn't care enough to do anything about it. The company had been in existence since 1868 and had a certain way of doing things, and I didn't see any major changes happening anytime soon.

During my corporate career, I would get bored very easily when the work was not challenging or when I felt I wasn't growing professionally. I was a quick learner, and once I had mastered a job I was ready to move on to the next best thing. If there were no opportunities to advance in sight, then I'd jump ship. I felt like I wasn't able to contribute as much as I wanted to and the work was just repetitive. The companies that I worked for didn't have much to offer me either, especially in terms of opportunities to develop further in my career. Most of the entrepreneurs that I've met or coached wouldn't have turned out to be good employees in the long run. I found some fulfillment by "job hopping" from one Fortune 500 company to the next, but it wasn't until I found my purpose that I was able to fulfill it within the context of my own business on my own terms. Entrepreneurship was calling my name.

Are you stuck in a mundane life or career? It may be time to shake things up a bit. Just as companies tolerate the status quo for too long, so can leaders—both personally and professionally. Find what you are passionate about and go do it. It will help you break out of monotony. You can't produce anything extraordinary just by existing in sameness.

I was once onsite at a client's office and one of the managers took me on a tour of the office building. The best way I can describe it is as a playground for adults. It was such a cool concept, and the place was obviously intentionally designed to facilitate change, creativity, and innovation. It was colorful with open spaces with different shapes and odd angles. The design seemed to be conducive for employees to explore new ideas and bring them to life. By its very appearance there was no room to maintain the status quo there.

COMPANY EXAMPLE: Spring Hill Entertainment (LeBron James)

James is an athlete, philanthropist, activist, businessman, and a brand, all-in-one. Why settle for one career path when you can use all of your gifts to create many? James has entered the fashion industry with the design of his signature Nike shoe, made cameo appearances as an actor in several movies and commercials, invested in many businesses, including Apple's acquisition of Beats Electronics, produced documentaries and web and TV series as a co-owner of Spring Hill Entertainment, founded *I Promise School,* and much more. He is the epitome of a serial entrepreneur who has defied the status quo by using his brands to promote good and to draw attention to social issues that are often controversial. Athletes are typically shunned for challenging the status quo because it is contrary to what the general public deems as acceptable. (LeBron James)

If you're going to continue to reinvent yourself, allow room for as many outlets as you need to express your creativity. Never allow anyone to put you in a box. The world needs your unique perspective to solving problems and producing change. The most pressing problems today are just waiting for someone to disrupt the status quo with a groundbreaking solution. It could be you.

CHAPTER 11

Mindset on Selling

Selling—The process of Exchanging Goods, Services, or Intellectual Property for Payment

Perhaps the most differentiating mindset between an entrepreneur and an employee lies in selling. Without sales, there is no income. Without income, there is no business. Entrepreneurs are intentional about selling their products, services, and information. There is no room for being coy when it comes to selling.

Most employees are not conditioned nor trained to sell. For employees, tasks are not always tied to the bottom line of an organization, so there is no incentive to sell. As an entrepreneur, sales must always directly connect to the tasks you do or money will be elusive. If you have never had a sales role, I strongly recommend that you take a sales course or read some books on sales. Long before I became an entrepreneur, I had a 100-percent commission-only sales job in the financial services industry where I sold mutual funds, annuities, life insurance, and more. If I didn't sell, I didn't eat. It was then that I learned to hone both my people skills and selling skills.

Selling is all about finding out what people want and offering it to them. It's that simple. It only gets complicated if you make it to be. It's not about convincing people to buy something that they don't need just so you can line your pockets. Of course you can do that, but you should want to operate with the highest level of integrity. I've been trained the wrong way to sell and I've been trained the right way too, so I can tell you which one will get you the best results and allow you to sleep at night.

My first experience with sales training was taught by an old-school guy who sold "by any means necessary." He called it prospecting. There were all kinds of crafty sales scripts I had to learn (which were totally unnatural to my personality). He taught us to present all of the unique features and benefits of the financial products to the potential clients. It wasn't until I was retrained the right way that I realized that I had been trained totally wrong.

I learned the right way to sell when I went for my certificate in an Integrity Selling class. I learned mostly about how to become a better listener so that I could pick up on buying signals from the potential clients. I learned how to ask the right questions that revealed to me exactly what the client needed before presenting them with any solutions. Take notice that I said solutions and not products. When you are selling, you are solving a problem, or otherwise meeting a need or giving clients what they already want. This is known as *consultative selling*. In a sales presentation, I talk only about 15 percent of the time and let the potential client talk the remaining 85 percent.

The key to selling with integrity is to be a principled person yourself. Customers can sniff out a snake oil salesperson from a mile away. Not only will you probably lose the sale, but chances are you will lose their respect and any chance of winning any future business with them. While there is an element of persuasion in sales, your primary focus should be on serving your customers well in a mutually beneficial way. In the age of social media, bad reviews often spread faster than the good ones, so don't stray from your values to make a dollar.

During a pitch or sales presentation, I take notes—sometimes written, other times only mental notes. By the time the potential clients are done speaking, I will have already come up with some solutions to the problems that they said they have. I usually present more than one option, because everyone loves options, and then I let them choose. I also discovered that people buy from those whom they like and trust. I'm a pretty affable person, so I usually just win people over by simply being myself. And this is how deals are closed!

Selling is a huge part of operating a profitable business. It's the one area of your business you cannot neglect. If you are fortunate enough to have enough startup capital to pay salaries, hiring a sales team would be a wise investment. If you can't just yet, then it would be to your advantage to learn sales techniques. There are lots of great sales training companies and conferences on selling.

For many people, including entrepreneurs whom I have coached, selling has a negative connotation that causes unnecessary trepidation. Selling is often associated with being pushy or dishonest. The reality is, when done the right way, this could not be further from the truth. Some don't like the notion of sales because they don't like to risk being rejected. They have created a false narrative in their minds that people don't want what they have to offer. Others just don't like the idea of promoting anything that has to do with themselves and feel that promoting their business, product, or service is somehow conceited.

Take a moment to think about any hang-up you might have about selling. Any fears about putting yourself, your brand, or your products and services out there will hinder the success of your business. You will need to confront and overcome the root causes of these issues so that they don't become stumbling blocks on your journey. Consider that selling is your announcement to the world that you have something great to offer that people want, need, and are willing pay for.

When selling, consistency and often times persistency are keys to closing deals and making money. This is where many fall short and give up too soon in the sales process. A potential customer may not be ready to buy immediately, but that doesn't mean he/she won't at a later date. A "not right now" response is not a "no." Therefore, having a follow-up process in place is key. I refer to this process as relationship management.

In your mind, you have to believe wholeheartedly in what you are selling. You have to believe that it is valuable enough that people will need or want what you have to offer. You have to be convinced that you might get a disproportionate amount of "no's" before you get one "yes." Your mind has to be strong enough to not take it personally or become discouraged if you didn't get that sale you wanted. There are other fish in the sea. Keep fishing! Others will see the value you are presenting and buy from you.

Market research and successful selling go hand-in-hand. If you've studied the market and you know your target market well, then you will be able to fine-tune your sales strategies to attract customers who are actually willing to buy. As you perfect this, you'll start selling to a more defined and more specific audience of potential customers, and your odds of closing deals will increase. Once you figure out what you are doing, your confidence will skyrocket and you'll become unstoppable!

It is worth noting that although having someone in your organization who has mastered sales techniques and strategies, sales is still a people business. When I teach my master class sessions, I always remind my students that business is 90 percent relational and only 10 percent transactional. If you don't learn how to build relationships with people, whether it's online or in person, you will likely fail in business. Learn how to master relationships first, then sales. Although many businesses see customers as tools to make money, that won't create loyal, long-term customers. Make a conscious effort to serve people well in your business. Sales without good customer service will ultimately end up creating a revolving door of customers in your business.

People can usually more easily remember a poor experience at a place of business than they can a good one. Can you recall a time that you had a bad encounter with a salesperson at a company? I can recall several. My most recent poor experience was with a timeshare salesperson who put his bestselling skills to work but then became condescending when I explained that I was not interested in upgrading. He was also not very forthcoming and omitted pertinent information that he should have disclosed. He forgot a key ingredient in the sales process, building relationships.

Whether you are a solopreneur or you have a team that you delegate to sell, proper training is a must or you will lose business. Selling requires a person who is comfortable putting himself/herself out there and can face the risk of being rejected. Here, I reiterate the importance to taking risks. Sales is such an integral part of doing business that any mental hang-ups or prejudice about sales can make a business to go under. The process goes like this: marketing ---> sales ---> revenue. Marketing is about being visible. Sales is about connecting with your clients and exchanging a product or service for money. Revenue is about the company's income, which should ultimately lead to profits.

Sales should be a daily business activity and should be made a priority. Many new business owners make the mistake of working so closely on their business and doing lots of administrative activities that they forget to close deals. Another rookie business blunder is mistaking social media followers for customers. While they may all be potential customers who might engage with your posts with likes or comments, converting them to loyal paying customers is when the real sales process begins.

Social media primarily serves as social proof for followers with vanity likes and comments. However, social media can be used as a form of marketing if the posts are leading its followers to buy something. There are also ways to advertise through paid social media sites to prevent your company's social media pages from bombarding followers with sales pitches all day. Soon, followers will get annoyed and will scroll pass your ads, or, worse, unfollow. Although social media can actually be used as an effective marketing and sales tool, let's not forget that it was first designed for connecting socially. Because business is based on building relationships, engaging with prospective customers online can help with fostering a larger and more loyal clientele.

As an entrepreneur, you have to think in terms of what your customer wants. Market research and website analytics can help you to understand your audience and their buying behavior. What you think is a great product, service, or information may not be so great for your target audience. Never blindly assume that you know what your customer wants or needs.

COMPANY EXAMPLE: Target

Target has a very smart sales strategy. It focuses on the three main business drivers: online sales, toys, and home goods. By focusing on growing in the areas that bring in the most revenue, it has achieved the highest sales growth in 2018 than it has seen in the previous 13 years. Target has seen a 41 percent increase in online sales alone. The retailer attributes their massive sales growth to being customer focused, adding more exclusive brands for customers ages 20 – 30, and adding celebrity home decor product lines. It's clear that Target understands what its customers want and need. (Bhattarai)

As you can see from the company example, Target, there is a certain psychology to the sales process. It is advantageous for any business owner to gain insight into this process to understand the way human behavior drives buying decisions. Thinking strategically of ways to connect with potential buyers is paramount to the sales process and to your overall success in business.

CHAPTER 12

Mindset on Self-determination

Self-determination—The Intrinsic and Relentless Willpower to Find a Way to Make Things Happen

Self-determination starts on the inside. No one can give it to you, but it can be developed. Do you have a history of giving up quickly? Do you struggle with not finishing what you started? Do you get discouraged easily? If so, then it's likely that you have not yet mastered self-determination.

Self-determination coupled with patience can be a powerful tool in your arsenal that you can pull out to help you stay the course when you are at a low point in your business and want to quit. It's not uncommon to face low moments in life or business. If you can be patient with the process and muster up enough self-determination, you can get past the rocky points. You often hear about the glamorous side of business like the flexibility, working from home, taking personal time off whenever you want. Don't be deceived by those social media photos of entrepreneurs on their private jets to Paris! No one likes to talk about the moments you want to throw in the towel. Some of those moments might include not making enough money, losing money, clients not paying invoices on time, business deals gone bad, bad business partnerships, difficult customers, fluctuating or unstable monthly income, and more.

COMPANY EXAMPLE: Virgin Group (Sir Richard Branson)

Most known for the successes of Virgin Atlantic Airlines, Virgin Mobile, Virgin Records, and Virgin Hotels, Sir Richard Branson has had more than his share of failures and setbacks. His most notable failures are Virgin Cola, Virgin Cars, Virgin Publishing, Virgin Clothing, and Virgin Brides, which all went defunct. After having some public scandals and the tragic losses of a close friend and his infant daughter, Branson has been able to survive them all and still manages to stay innovative and create new companies under his conglomerate. Virgin Cargo, Virgin Holidays, Virgin Money, Virgin Active, Virgin Healthcare, and Virgin Media are also some of the other brands created by Branson. In 2004, Branson launched Virgin Galactic, a spaceflight company that develops commercial space crafts. (Richard Branson)

The ability to keep going even when you don't feel like it is not an easy task, especially if you've been knocked down and repeatedly discouraged. However, it is doable if your reason for continuing is greater than the pain you have to endure to reach your goals. Getting in the habit of pushing past your emotions or discomfort is what will develop the discipline needed to become self-determined. Internally, self-determined people have a strong foundation of internal strength that they draw from somewhere. For some, achieving a particular goal is self-gratifying or they have something to prove to themselves. For others, it could be drawing strength from something less self-serving, like faith, belief systems, spirituality, or from the satisfaction that the end result will contribute something great to this world.

In order to be self-determined, you must first be able to identify what drives you. For some, it's getting out of poverty. For others, it could be getting others out of poverty. You might be inspired to solve a particular problem that changes the world. Perhaps you have a strong desire to influence the world with your gifts. Maybe you see something missing that is badly needed on this earth, for example, good, morally sound leadership, and you have a strong desire to fill that leadership void in order to make a difference.

Your passion and your gifts are a powerful duo that can reveal a lot about your inner workings. They are both very closely knit to your life's purpose. When your purpose and your vocation align, you are then doing what you were born to do. Once you arrive at this point, being self-determined becomes much easier. Your purpose is what drives you and convinces you that have something to look forward to waking up for every day. It activates your life.

It is easier to persevere when the work that you do in your business is meaningful, fulfilling, and connected to your life's purpose in some way. What naturally drives you is what intrinsically motivates you. Once you identify it and tap into it, it would be wise not to deviate from it. In more simple terms, do what you love. Do what comes natural to you. Do what you are gifted to do. To go against these things is like trying to swim upstream.

One of the things I am passionate about besides giving strategies that grow businesses is traveling. I discovered that it's just good for my soul. So naturally, I wanted to design the work that I do in my companies around my love for traveling. When you own the company, you can make decisions that are personally fulfilling. If you go against your purpose, you will likely find it to be challenging to maintain lasting determination.

You won't know how determined you are until you are put in situations that test your resilience. Like a muscle, each time you use your determination, it will get stronger. Throughout the course of running your business, you'll have plenty of occasions to exercise it. Running a business has an unintended way of developing your personal character. As such, you will grow and your capacity to lead will also. This will in turn have a positive impact on your company. Your judgment and decision-making abilities will improve, and so will your single-mindedness, because determination also helps you to focus on the task at hand.

Entrepreneurs don't wait around for others to motivate or inspire them. Their motivation is usually intrinsic, and, when necessary, they will proactively seek out what they need to propel themselves to the next level. This is one of the characteristics that make them so unique. Taking charge of their own success is a way of life.

Since self-determination is so closely tied to the inner workings of the mind, there are things that you can begin doing to strengthen your resolve and to become unwavering in your approach to business. Start with the present and forget about your past disappointments, discouragements, and defeats. Focus on what you can do today. Self-determined people take actions and hold themselves accountable. Make a promise to yourself and keep it.

MINDSET EXERCISE 12.1—Holding Yourself Accountable

As a firm believer that you don't truly believe something unless you act on it, I have provided the following exercise for you to demonstrate that you can do anything that you put your mind to. Fill in the blanks in the column on the right. Choose the goals for your current or future business that you will accomplish within the specified time frame. Check "done" after accomplishing those goals.

Done☐

Today I will . . .		
In the next 7 days I will . . .		
In the next 30 days I will . . .		
In the next 6 months I will . . .		
In the next 12 months I will . . .		

Be intentional about referring to these goals until they are completed. Push yourself to accomplish these goals and seek help from someone if you need it. This is a large of part of developing your self-determination. You can discipline yourself to do almost anything that you fully commit yourself to do.

Final Words

Cultivating an entrepreneurial mindset is a necessary process to prepare your mind for the journey of working for yourself. It requires commitment to this process as you develop the type of thinking that will lead you to begin making the types of decisions that successful entrepreneurs make. Entrepreneurs don't think like employees, which is what makes them so unique and a minority in this world. The 12 fundamental areas of an entrepreneur's mindset were expounded upon with real examples of how I and other entrepreneurs applied entrepreneurial thinking to actions and business decisions and the outcomes of those decisions. The Mindset Exercises were designed for you to do the work that's essential to develop the mental capacity to make the right decisions that will create and sustain a flourishing business venture.

If you have only worked for others as an employee and have had little to no exposure to business owners, this process of adjusting your thinking to become more entrepreneurial can be quite a paradigm shift because you will have to be unindoctrinated. If you are naturally wired to work for yourself, you will likely apply the concepts in this book with more ease. Everyone's journey will be different. There are many variables that shape the way an individual thinks, and, as such, there will be a myriad of ways to achieve an entrepreneurial mindset.

I've cultivated my entrepreneurial mindset over the course of several years. I surrounded myself with more entrepreneurs and people who supported me and my dreams. I distanced myself from those who were on an opposite trajectory in life. I cut off small thinkers, stagnant people who had no curiosity about the world around them, dream snatchers, and haters. I immersed myself in books, articles, videos, webinars, and business conferences that were created by successful entrepreneurs for entrepreneurs. I said "no" to opportunities and all distractions that would have caused me to deviate from my business goals. Conversely, I deliberately said "yes" to business opportunities that forced me to go well beyond my comfort zone and pushed me to grow my business and also develop personally. I was, and I am, laser-focused on living my life's purpose and impacting the lives of others through my gifts, talents, skill sets, and abilities in the marketplace.

How quickly you make the mindset shift is contingent upon your willingness, the amount of experience you've had working for yourself, or being closely connected to other entrepreneurs. There is a possibility that you decide that entrepreneurship is not for you and that you are better off taking a different path. Entrepreneurship is not for everyone, although everyone can monetize their gifts or skill sets in some way if they choose. Choose the path that aligns with your purpose and your passion.

MINDSET EXERCISE 12.2—Mindset Adjustment

As a final exercise, fill in the following table to reflect on the ways you need to adjust your mindset to think more like an entrepreneur. Based on what you have learned about yourself regarding the 12 fundamental areas, list specific ways or things that you could do to adjust how you think. For example, if you are very risk-averse, list at least one action that you could take to push yourself to overcome the risk.

Fundamental Areas	Ways I Need to Adjust
Risk	
Leadership	
Vision	
Pioneering/Innovation	
Obstacles	
Change	
Failure	
Work	
Creativity	
Status Quo	
Selling	
Self-determination	

Questions to ponder: What did you learn about yourself? How will you apply the lessons that you have learned from what you've read? What implications does what you read have for your choice about whether or not to pursue entrepreneurship?

Your attitude and beliefs about these 12 fundamental areas in the context of entrepreneurship will determine how well you will be able to take on the challenges that you will encounter on your journey as an entrepreneur. If you are willing to do the work to cultivate your mind, it can be life-changing, not only for your business but also for your life in general. The results will be the development of a mental fortitude that cannot be shaken, a positive outlook in the midst of troubles, the resilience to see your dreams become a reality, and giving yourself permission to be your most authentic and best self regardless of the circumstances. This process is intended to challenge you and to draw out your potential and your best qualities as a leader and an entrepreneur.

Whatever the state of your current mindset, it became that way because it was cultivated over the course of several years. In general, people are not always aware of exactly what has shaped their way of thinking or how it happened because it happens little-by-little, day-by-day, year-by-year. Then, one day you realize that you have a whole set of beliefs that shape how you function in this world and how you view it. Subconsciously, your beliefs have already been developed and continue to shape who you think you are and what you believe you are capable of doing.

Cultivating an entrepreneurial mindset is no different than how your mind has already been cultivated to be the way it is today, except that the process is now intentional instead of subliminal. Now that you are attentive to how you can develop your mindset, you can apply these principles to help shape the way you think specifically as an entrepreneur. Your mind is the springboard to your success, so be purposeful and careful how you nurture it. Be willing to unlearn things that have caused you to believe things that are detrimental to your success.

And now what? The next steps that you can take to cultivate an entrepreneurial mindset and to apply the 12 principles discussed in this book are up to you, but here are some suggestions:

- Carefully review your answers to the Mindset Exercises and the Assessment and draw out any patterns you might observe about yourself. If you notice any weak areas in your thinking that appear more often than others, that is an indication that those areas need more of your attention to work on them for improvement. Those are the areas I suggest you tackle first and push yourself to do better.

- If you have a vision for starting a business, write it down first. Then, think of other like-minded people with whom you can share your vision, such as a mentor, a trusted advisor, a business person, or potential business partners. This will put momentum behind what's in your head and also solicit the professional opinions and help from people who can vet your business plans and encourage you to move forward. It's a small step, but it shows intention.
- Start building your network. Having access to the right people can help advance your business ideas. Connect with the entrepreneur hubs and ecosystems online, on campus, and in your community. If you have access to funders (venture capitalists, private investors, microlenders, grant organizations, etc.), startup competitions, business accelerators, incubators and innovations centers, community development programs, Small Business Development Centers, entrepreneur work spaces, and other local skills training organizations for entrepreneurs, then make use of these resources.
- If you already have a business, identify any of the 12 areas in your thinking that have hindered you or your business and take deliberate actions to master these areas.

Warning! One thing is for certain. As you begin to think more entrepreneurially and do what successful entrepreneurs do, not everyone will be happy about your new change (but that's really none of your business!) Just be aware that the world that entrepreneurs live in is one of its own and very different than the world in which nonentrepreneurs live. The drive, sacrifices, and time that it will take for you to succeed on this journey might alienate you from your current circle of friends and even well-meaning family members who might suggest that you should come back down to earth and get a regular job like everyone else. I'm not suggesting that you become reckless in following your dream and destroy your relationships along the way. However, you should just prepare yourself for the likelihood of changes in relationships. It's a price that many, if not all, entrepreneurs have had to pay at some point on this journey.

There is also a much larger context in which this book fits. The world is moving more and more toward remote work, digital nomadic work and lifestyles, freelancing, online marketing, and remote startup companies. You should care about cultivating an entrepreneurial mindset regardless of whether you decide to run a Fortune 500 company or do freelance gigs to create an additional income stream. Even the global workforce is beginning to embrace technology, and the demands for flexible and work-from-home arrangements are increasing in almost every industry, with some companies moving towards a 100 percent virtual workforce. Therefore, employees are expected to think entrepreneurially by managing their own time or schedules, working independently, and having more autonomy over their work as they work from home. With an entrepreneurial mindset, you become an asset to an organization, whether it's yours or someone else's.

One implication is that you can take advantage of finding skilled contractors and employees from all over the world to work in your business. You have access to a global talent pool at your fingertips. At the time that I am writing this book, my companies are 100 percent virtual by my design. My teams and business partners are located in seven countries across four continents. This is proof that the world is now more conducive to entrepreneurship than ever. The barriers to entry are almost nonexistent, and technology has removed most geographical boundaries with the help of devices, apps, and the internet which can connect with almost anyone instantly. It's important to take notice of these trends so that you can take advantage of this opportunity to allow your gifts and talents to reach the world and to prosper.

Many people are simply getting tired of trading hours for dollars in a conventional 9-to-5 job. Employers are providing less and less benefits and, in many cases, are offering no pensions or significant retirement contributions, especially in the United States. Employees' wages are often stagnant, even with inflation and the increase in experience or skill sets gained over time. Work hours are frequently not flexible enough for those who have unpredictable family situations and for those who already have children or want to have children someday. Your personal time off and vacation hours as an employee are totally at the discretion of the employer. And as such, many are considering entrepreneurship as both a viable career and lifestyle change.

There could not be a better time to cultivate an entrepreneurial mindset. During times of political upheaval and economic instability worldwide, knowing what value you can bring to the world apart from dependency on an employer will give you a great advantage in the midst of economic recessions and downturns. An entrepreneurial mindset creates an ability to monetize skill sets in any environment. It also activates your ability to continuously reinvent yourself whenever necessary, as well as create multiple streams of income that will give you financial stability. Using the tools in this book to cultivate your entrepreneurial mindset, your mind can become powerful and your opportunities limitless.

APPENDIX

Mindset Assessment Scoring Guide

Odd number questions answered with a Yes = 1 point
Even number questions answered with a Yes = 4 points
Odd number questions answered with a No = 3 points
Even number questions answered with a No = 1 point

The highest score possible is 105 points. The lowest score possible is 30.

Score = 30–48—The Smooth Sailor

Your preferences indicate that you enjoy a more conventional approach to your work. Risk is mostly uncomfortable for you, and currently you are better suited to a more defined work environment that has routines, structure, and predictability. You prefer not to rock the boat and have a "if it ain't broke don't fix it" mentality. The status quo probably doesn't bother you much, and you will likely find great fulfillment in working for someone else as an employee.

Score = 49–67—The Team Player

You show that minimal risk is welcome in your career journey. Although you are most inclined to safety and security, you appear to take on occasional but very calculated risks that don't stretch you too far outside of your comfort zone. You will likely rise to the occasion when required, and, as such, you fit well into a team environment within the workplace.

Score = 68–86—The Intrapreneur Leader

You display some characteristics of an entrepreneur, which might lend itself very well while leading a group of people within the organization you work for. If you desire to start a business, with the right development, you could do well as an entrepreneur. You are not a stranger to risk, but you probably don't thrive on it. People can depend on you and look to you for guidance because of your outlook on getting things done.

Score = 87–105—**The Enterprising Boss**

You demonstrate a mindset that is conducive to succeeding as an entrepreneur. If you are not currently a business owner, you should strongly consider the path of entrepreneurship. Your capacity for taking on a higher-than-average amount of risk and your leadership attributes are qualities that are necessary for running a business and making your mark on this world. You are not guided by fear and are definitely not a follower. A traditional 9-to-5 job will stifle your creativity and place limitations on your potential.

References

Beauty Independent. 2018. "Volition Beauty Allows Individual Consumers To Create Products With Major Mass Appeal." *Beauty Independent*. July 13, 2018. https://www.beautyindependent.com/volition-beauty-crowdsourced-products-qvc-sephora

Belanger, L. 2018. "10 of the Most Successful Black Entrepreneurs." *Entrepreneur*. February 16, 2018. https://www.entrepreneur.com/slideshow/309108#2

Bhattarai, A. 2018. "Target's Sales Growth Is at a 13-year High, Thanks to Demand for Toys and Home Goods." *The Washington Post*. August 22, 2018. https://www.washingtonpost.com/business/2018/08/22/targets-sales-are-year-high-thanks-demand-toys-home-goods/?noredirect=on&utm_term=.4054aba44e58

Bloomberg. 2014. "Alibaba IPO: Jack Ma's Original Sales Pitch in 1999." *YouTube*. September 08, 2014. https://www.youtube.com/watch?v=Up9-C4_8dVo

CB Insights Research. 2018. "When Corporate Innovation Goes Bad - The 101 Biggest Product Failures Of All Time." *CB Insights Research*. December 19, 2018. https://www.cbinsights.com/research/corporate-innovation-product-fails/?utm_source=CB%2BInsights%2BNewsletter&utm_campaign=854aa52ce9-Top_Research_Briefs_12_22_2018&utm_medium=email&utm_term=0_9dc0513989-854aa52ce9-91777577

Chargify. 2016. "6 Companies That Succeeded by Changing Their Business Model." *Chargify Blog*. August 04, 2016. https://www.chargify.com/blog/6-companies-that-succeeded-by-changing-their-business-model

Council, Young Entrepreneur. 2018. "23 Trends That Will Shake The Business World In 2018." *Forbes*. March 15, 2018. https://www.forbes.com/sites/theyec/2018/01/10/23-trends-that-will-shake-the-business-world-in-2018/#df53a46583f9

Cuellar, T. 2018. "Leading With Love: An Unconventional Approach To Leadership." *Forbes*. June 29, 2018. https://www.forbes.com/sites/

forbescoachescouncil/2018/06/29/leading-with-love-an-unconventional-approach-to-leadership/#1284651d1123

Edwards, B. 2017. "Unraveling The Enigma of Nintendo's Virtual Boy, 20 Years Later." *Fast Company*. February 02, 2017. https://www.fastcompany.com/3050016/unraveling-the-enigma-of-nintendos-virtual-boy-20-years-later

Elide Fire Ball NZ. n.d. "The World's First Self-activating Mobile Fire Suppression Ball." *Elide Fire Ball NZ*. http://elidefireball.co.nz

Glassdoor. 2018. "Top CEOs." *Glassdoor*. https://www.glassdoor.com/Award/Top-CEOs-LST_KQ0,8.htm

Ibekwe, D. 2018. "This Sea-craft Looks like a Plane, Has a Race-car Engine, and Docks like a Boat." *Business Insider*. March 4, 2018. https://www.businessinsider.com/sea-craft-looks-like-a-plane-docks-boat-airfish-8-widgetworks-2018-3?r=UK&IR=T

Krupnick, E. 2013. "USPS Clothing Line, Rain Heat & Snow, Is Postal Service's Latest Foray into Fashion." *HuffPost*. February 20, 2013. https://www.huffpost.com/entry/usps-clothing-line-rain-heat-snow_n_2725156

Loraine. 2018. "15 Companies That Made A Miraculous Comeback After Near Extinction." *Self Made*. February 11, 2018. https://self-made.io/8-companies-made-miraculous-comeback-near-extinction/4183/5

Mullins, J. 2014. *The Customer-funded Business: Start, Finance, or Grow Your Company with Your Customers' Cash*. Hoboken, NJ: John Wiley & Sons.

Olson, B. "Cloud Communications Success." 6 Ways the Cloud Is Changing Business Communication. *Coredial*. https://success.coredial.com/blog/calculated-risk-great-rewards-top-entrepreneurs

Profit With Purpose. https://www.profitwithpurpose.co.uk

Spredfast. 2018. "The 2018 Social Audience Guide." *Spredfast*. https://www.spredfast.com/social-media-tips/social-media-demographics-current

Valentine, M. 2018. "9 Incredibly Successful Entrepreneurs Who All Failed Big Before Winning Bigger." *Goalcast*. February 22, 2018. https://www-goalcast-com.cdn.ampproject.org/v/s/www.goalcast.com/2018/02/22/successful-entrepreneurs-who-failed-big/amp/?amp_js_v=a2&_gsa=1&usqp=mq331AQECAFYAQ%3D

%3D#aoh=15458810670670&_ct=1545881263688&referrer=ht
tps%3A%2F%2Fwww.google.com&_tf=From%20%251%24s&sh
are=https%3A%2F%2Fwww.goalcast.com%2F2018%2F02%2F22
%2Fsuccessful-entrepreneurs-who-failed-big%2F

Wikipedia. 2019a. "Oprah Winfrey." *Wikipedia.* January 4, 2019. https://
en.wikipedia.org/wiki/Oprah_Winfrey

Wikipedia. 2019b. "Richard Branson." *Wikipedia.* January 06, 2019.
https://en.wikipedia.org/wiki/Richard_Branson.

About the Author

Dynamite in a small package, fearless, and inspiring are just a few words to describe **Tamiko L. Cuellar**, the CEO and the founder of Pursue Your Purpose LLC and Africa Trade Partners LLC. She is a proven leader in the global business community and has been invited to speak at the U.S. Embassy in Namibia, the University of Namibia (Africa), the University of South Africa, Microsoft, First Bank, the City of St. Louis (United States), chambers of commerce, governments, corporations, churches, and conferences throughout the world. She has been a regular contributor to *Forbes.com* and *The Huffington Post*, and has been featured on *Good Morning Namibia*, *Wake Up Nigeria*, *Ghana Broadcasting Corporation*, *One Africa TV*, *The African Independent*, *The Republikein*, and several other international media houses.

Tamiko was nominated for the 2013 Business Influencer Award, and in 2016, she was recognized by *The Women's Business Journals* as a Woman on the Move. In 2016–2017, she was appointed as a mentor to emerging entrepreneurs in Africa as part of Tony Elumelu's Entrepreneurship Program. She served as an adjunct professor of entrepreneurship/small business management at City Vision University. She has taught or facilitated in universities in the U.S., Ghana, Namibia, and South Africa. She is a member of the National Association of Professional Women (NAPW) and the Forbes Coaches Council. She oversees a growing team which operates in seven countries spanning across four continents. Tamiko is also the president and founder of Africa Trade Partners, a company that provides services to facilitate trade between the United States and Sub-Saharan African businesses.

Born into a broken family who lived in low-income housing projects, growing up in poverty in a crime-ridden neighborhood, and getting educated in the underperforming school district of East St. Louis, Illinois, she considers herself to be a flower that was determined to rise from the cracks of concrete to grow and flourish. She went on to obtain three business degrees from the University of Missouri-Columbia on a full academic scholarship, the University of Phoenix, and City Vision University, respectively, and has had a successful and adventurous career helping to secure over $30 million revenue, training employees, and obtaining millions of investment dollars in corporate America prior to launching her own companies.

Pursue Your Purpose LLC is a global firm that coaches aspiring and emerging women with strategies to successfully transition into entrepreneurship and to grow. With her unique approach and methodologies to train and help entrepreneurs to monetize their gifts and align their life purpose with business and profits, she has helped thousands around the globe, mixing inspiration with cutting-edge business strategies to help emerging entrepreneurs reach their next level. Pursue Your Purpose LLC provides live and virtual conferences, strategy sessions, group and private coaching, workshops, corporate training, and books. Tamiko is also the bestselling author of *20 Beautiful Women: 20 More Stories That Will Heal Your Soul, Ignite Your Passion and Inspire Your Divine Purpose* (Volume 2); *101 Tools to Take Your Startup or Solopreneur Business to the Next Level*; and *Own Your Brilliance!—A Woman's Guide to Hiring Herself.* For corporations, colleges, conferences, churches, radio, TV interviews, and more, Tamiko is available as a guest speaker, facilitator, and trainer on topics related to entrepreneurship, women's empowerment, leadership development, and exporting from Sub-Saharan Africa into the United States. For booking inquiries, email booking@PursueYourPurpose.com.

Index

OTHER TITLES IN THE ENTREPRENEURSHIP AND SMALL BUSINESS MANAGEMENT COLLECTION

Scott Shane, Case Western University, *Editor*

- *Startup Strategy Humor: Democratizing Startup Strategy* by Rajesh K. Pillania
- *The Leadership Development Journey: How Entrepreneurs Develop Leadership Through Their Lifetime* by Jen Vuhuong
- *Getting to Market With Your MVP: How to Achieve Small Business and Entrepreneur Success* by J.C. Baker
- *Can You Run Your Business With Blood, Sweat, and Tears? Volume I: Blood* by Stephen Elkins-Jarrett and Nick Skinner
- *Can You Run Your Business With Blood, Sweat, and Tears? Volume II: Sweat* by Stephen Elkins-Jarrett and Nick Skinner
- *Can You Run Your Business With Blood, Sweat, and Tears? Volume III: Tear* by Stephen Elkins-Jarrett and Nick Skinner
- *Family Business Governance: Increasing Business Effectiveness and Professionalism* by Keanon J. Alderson
- *Department of Startup: Why Every Fortune 500 Should Have One* by Ivan Yong Wei Kit and Sam Lee
- *The Rainmaker: Start-Up to Conglomerate* by Jacques Magliolo
- *Get on Board: Earning Your Ticket to a Corporate Board Seat* by Olga V. Mack
- *From Vision to Decision: A Self-Coaching Guide to Starting a New Business* by Dana K. Dwyer

Announcing the Business Expert Press Digital Library

Concise e-books business students need for classroom and research

This book can also be purchased in an e-book collection by your library as

- a one-time purchase,
- that is owned forever,
- allows for simultaneous readers,
- has no restrictions on printing, and
- can be downloaded as PDFs from within the library community.

Our digital library collections are a great solution to beat the rising cost of textbooks. E-books can be loaded into their course management systems or onto students' e-book readers.

The **Business Expert Press** digital libraries are very affordable, with no obligation to buy in future years. For more information, please visit **www.businessexpertpress.com/librarians**. To set up a trial in the United States, please email **sales@businessexpertpress.com**.